THE PSALMS FOR CHILDREN

60 Object Lessons on the Psalms
Series B

ELDON WEISHEIT

AUGSBURG Publishing House • Minneapolis

THE PSALMS FOR CHILDREN/SERIES B
60 Object Lessons

Copyright © 1984   Augsburg Publishing House

Library of Congress Cataloging in Publicaton Data

Weisheit, Eldon.
    THE PSALMS FOR CHILDREN, SERIES B.

    1. Bible.   O.T.   Psalms—Children's sermons.
I. Title.
BS1430.4.W453   1984   2234206   84-18562
ISBN 0-8066-2096-X

Manufactured in the U.S.A.   APH 10-5304

1   2   3   4   5   6   7   8   9   0   1   2   3   4   5   6   7   8   9

Contents

Preface

Psalm 34:11 is a good test to guide the person who wishes to preach children's sermons. It says, "Come, my young friends, and listen to me, and I will teach you to have reverence for the Lord."

When you invite the children forward in a worship service, or when you walk in front of a class of children, you have a goal. You want them to hear the message of God's love in Jesus Christ. You want them to listen, not just as a sign of respect for you or for the place of worship, but to hear the words of forgiveness, grace, hope, and eternal life through Jesus Christ.

For the children to hear the message, you must speak it. And the message must be spoken to their world. For the message to be of value to them, it must be true in two ways. It must be true to what has happened in the death and resurrection of Christ. It must also be true to what is happening in the lives of the children. Forgiveness must be applied to their sins. Hope must reach their worries. Joy must spring out of their experiences of love and success.

Psalm 34:11 offers another guide for the preacher of children's sermons. It says, "I will teach you to have reverence for the Lord." All other translations I checked remain with "fear of the Lord." I readily grant that according to the dictionary "fear" is a good translation. For those who know the church use of "fear," it is a beautiful thought. But it is not the language of children—or adults—outside the church. The word *fear* brings back to our mouths the taste of the fruit of the tree of the knowledge of good and evil. That type of fear makes us join Adam and Eve in hiding from God.

The message for the preacher of children's sermons is this: Do not teach your hearers a special language so they can understand what you are saying. Instead give them the message not only in the language that they understand but that they may also use to pass the good news on to people who will never sit in the pew to hear your sermons. Your preaching will go far beyond the church building or classroom if you give it in ideas and words that your hearers can use to tell others.

Again, my thanks to the people of Fountain of Life Lutheran Church, Tucson, Arizona, for encouraging me in this type of preaching and to Mary Lou Schram for being my overly qualified proofreader.

Eldon Weisheit

Bring Us Back, O God!

THE WORLD

Bring us back, O God!
Show us your mercy, and we will be saved!
Psalm 80:3 (First Sunday in Advent)

THE WORLD

A sandwich, a picture of a house, a picture of parents, the manger and baby from a crèche

---

Gail was angry at her parents. She thought they loved her brother more than they loved her. She thought they made her do too many chores around the house. So Gail ran away from home.

After Gail had been away from home for several hours she began to worry. She wondered if she had done the right thing. She wanted to go back home. What do you think made Gail want to go home? Was she hungry? *(Show sandwich.)* Did she think about the snack her mother had left for her in the refrigerator? Or did she want to be back in her own house again? *(Show picture of house.)* Was she thinking about her bed and the TV? Or do you think Gail thought about her parents? *(Show picture of parents.)* Did she know that they were worried about her? Did she know they loved her?

Which of these three things would you show Gail to make her want to go home again? Maybe Gail thought about all three. She would be hungry. Her home would be a safe place. And she would remember she had food and a home because her parents loved her. That love would welcome her home.

Because we sin we also turn away from God. We

sometimes feel about God the way Gail felt about her parents. Maybe God doesn't love us as much as he loves someone else. God asks us to do too much. So we run away from God.

Psalm 80 says, "Bring us back, O God! Show us your mercy, and we will be saved!" The person who wrote this psalm felt he was far away from God. But he was like Gail: he wanted to go back home to God again.

We talked about the things that made Gail want to go back home. When you feel you are far away from God, what makes you want to go back to him again? The psalm writer told us what he missed about God. He said, "Show us your mercy, and we will be saved!" He remembered that God was merciful. He knew God was loving and forgiving.

Now I want to show you something to remind you of the mercy of God. See this manger with the baby in it? Today is the first Sunday in Advent. We are getting ready to celebrate Christmas. We will tell the story and sing the songs about the birth of Jesus.

When Jesus was born, God showed mercy to us. God showed that he loved us. God sent Jesus to be not only the baby born in the manger but also the Savior who died on the cross to pay for our sins.

We celebrate Advent and Christmas every year to remind ourselves of the mercy of God. If you ever feel that you are far away from God, remember his mercy. You too can say, "Bring us back, O God! Show us your mercy, and we will be saved!"

He Made His Own Path

THE WORD
Righteousness will go before the Lord
and prepare the path for him.
                    Psalm 85:13 (Second Sunday in Advent)

THE WORLD
A roll of paper towels

Robin, will you help me today? I want you to go from here to there. *(Indicate a place on the same floor level as you are standing.)* That sounds easy, but there is one special rule. The rule is: Your feet cannot touch the floor between here and there. That means that neither your shoes, nor your socks, nor your bare feet can touch the floor. Can you do it?

You may think it is impossible to do what I asked, but I'll show you one way to do it. Use this *(roll of paper towels)*. Put the roll in front of you and stand on the first towel. Now with one foot push the roll ahead of you. Then take another step. See—you are making your own path as you go. Your feet are not touching the floor because you are walking on your path. Not only have you done what I asked you to do, but you have also made it possible for the rest of us to do it. You have left a path that we can follow and also walk on without touching the floor.

When Jesus came to live on earth, he also had a job that seemed impossible. He is God. That means he is holy and righteous. But he came to earth to be a human being like us. We are all sinners. He had to stay holy to be God. But he had to walk the way of sinners to be one with us. How could he do that?

The psalm for today tells us how he did it. It says, "Righteousness will go before the Lord and prepare the path for him." When Jesus came to earth he brought his righteousness, that means his goodness and holiness, with him. Jesus used his righteousness like Robin used the roll of paper towels. He made a path for himself and walked on it. He was always standing on his goodness, but he lived with people who were sinners.

Jesus made a path of goodness everywhere he went. He went to sick people with his goodness and he healed them. He went to poor people with his goodness and he helped them. He made a path of goodness to all sinners. That path led him to a cross where he died to pay for the sins of the world. By his death he brought his goodness to all sinners. Jesus' path of righteousness led him to a grave, but it also led him out of the grave. He rose from the dead and made a path back to heaven.

See the path Robin made? It is still there so any of us can walk on it as she did. Our feet would not touch the floor. Jesus also left a path of righteousness on earth. He gave us his goodness. We can follow his path. We start on his path when we go to the stable where he was born. We follow him as we live with people and share in the lives of others as he did. Even when we die we will be following his path. His path leads through death to heaven.

Something You Can't Buy

THE WORD

Mary said, "He has filled the hungry with good things,
and sent the rich away with empty hands."

Luke 1:53 (Third Sunday in Advent)

THE WORLD

An orange and 50 cents

═══

Two children go into a grocery store. They see this
orange. *(Show orange.)* One says, "That orange looks
good. I'm hungry." The other says, "Here's 50 cents.
I'd like that orange." Which child gets the orange?
The one with the money, right? Of course, the store
has oranges to sell, not to give away. The one who
buys the orange gets it.

Now suppose the orange is at your grandmother's
house. She has already bought it at the store. You see
the orange and say, "That orange looks good. I'm
hungry." A telephone repairman is also at your grandmother's house. He sees the orange and says, "Here's
50 cents. I'd like that orange." Who do you think
would get the orange? I think your grandmother
would give it to you rather than sell it to the repairman. She did not buy the orange in order to sell it.
She bought it for her family, and you are a part of
the family.

Now think of this orange as being the gospel of
Jesus Christ. The gospel is the message of God's love
for us. The gospel tells us Jesus died for our sins. It
tells us Jesus is with us now and will be forever.

Who do you think gets the gospel? Does it go to
the one who says, "Here's money. I'd like to be

saved."? Or does it go to the one who says, "I am glad you love me, Jesus. Please forgive me."?

The Bible reading for today tells us who gets what Jesus has for us. Mary, his mother, told us about Jesus even before he was born. She said, "He has filled the hungry with good things, and sent the rich away with empty hands."

Mary knew Jesus would not run a store to sell what he had. He did not come to earth to sell his love to those who had money or power. He would give to those who needed what he had. They would be a part of his family. He would send the rich away. Jesus loves all people, so he loves rich people too. But rich people cannot buy Jesus' love. If they think they can buy from Jesus or if they think they are first in line, he will send them away.

Jesus came to give God's love to all people. Poor people know they need God's help. They accept the gift and thank him for it. Sometimes rich people do not want to accept a gift. They want to pay their own way. But they cannot buy God's love.

While you are a child, you know how to accept gifts. You do not think you can pay for all the things your parents and others give you. When you become an adult, you will still be God's child. You will not buy from God. He will give to you. What God has for you is so great, no money can buy it. God gives you his Son to be your Savior.

A Gift That Lasts Forever

THE WORD

You [the Lord] said,
"I have made a convenant with the man I chose;
I have promised my servant David,
'A descendant of yours will always be king;
I will preserve your dynasty forever.' "
Psalm 89:3-4 (Fourth Sunday in Advent)

THE WORLD

A box of candy and a pair of earrings

Scott went shopping to buy a Christmas present for his mother. He looked at many different things. He checked the price tags to see which ones he could buy with the money in his pocket. Finally he had to choose between these two gifts. He could buy either this candy or these earrings. *(Show candy and earrings.)* He knew his mother liked candy. It would be a special treat. He also knew his mother liked earrings. He thought these would look nice on her.

Both gifts were nice. She would enjoy either. Scott had a hard time making up his mind. Then he thought about next summer when the family would go on vacation. The candy would be gone by then. But his mother would still have the earrings. He decided he wanted to give his mother a gift that would last a long time. So he bought the earrings.

God plans to give you a gift for Christmas. He wants you to have a special friend. You may have many different friends. There are friends at school, friends at church, friends on your ball team or at Scouts. Some friends are like the box of candy. They

14

last only for a while. One person may be your friend only for a day. It's OK to have a friend for only a short time, just like it's OK to have a gift that lasts only a short time.

But sometimes you want a friend that lasts a long time. You may now have some friends who will be your friends the rest of your life. But the friend God wants to give you at Christmas will be your friend even longer than that. Listen to what the Lord said in Psalm 89: "I have made a covenant with the man I chose; I have promised my servant David, 'A descendant of yours will always be king; I will preserve your dynasty forever.'"

When God chose a friend for you, he picked one who would last forever. God made a promise to King David that one of David's sons would be a king who would rule forever.

Jesus was born to Mary and Joseph who were descendants of King David. Jesus became a king—not just the king of one country for a while, but king for everyone forever. He became a king because he battled against sin and death when he was crucified on the cross. He won the victory when he rose from the dead. Now he rules with God the Father over heaven and earth.

Jesus, the King, is your friend. He is the gift God gives to you. The earrings Scott bought for his mother will last a long time. But she might lose one, or they might be stolen or broken. Scott's gift to his mother will last a long time, but not forever. God's gift to you is forever. Jesus is with you now, and he always will be.

Earth, Be Glad!

THE WORD

The Lord is king! Earth, be glad! . . .
Light shines on the righteous,
and gladness on the good.

Psalm 97:1a, 11 (Christmas Day)

THE WORLD

The figures from a crèche

Do you know what these are? *(Show animals from the crèche.)* This is a sheep, this a donkey, this a camel. Why do you think I have little statues of animals today? Do they belong in a play zoo? Am I going to play farm? Of course not. These animals are from a manger scene. At another time of the year you might wonder why I have toy animals. But at Christmas time you know why. As soon as this *(show the figure of the baby)* is added, you know why I have the animals. Jesus was born in a stable. Animals were there.

We do not think about other animals that lived 2000 years ago. But we remember these because Jesus was there. The baby made the animals important too.

Do you know who these are? *(Show people from the crèche.)* This is a shepherd. These are the Wise Men. Here are Mary and Joseph. These people lived 2000 years ago. They would have been forgotten except for one thing. Jesus *(show the baby figure)* became a part of their lives. He lived in a home with Mary and Joseph. The shepherds and the Wise Men saw him for only a short time. But Jesus was a part of their lives.

16

Each of these figures *(put the crèche together)* became important because Jesus is in the center. The baby who was born in the stable became the man who died on the cross to pay for the sins of the world. The one who died on the cross rose again and still lives. Because he is still alive we also remember those who were with him at the time of his birth—even the animals.

Jesus came for the whole world, not just for those who were in Bethlehem at the time of his birth. Psalm 97 says, "The Lord is king! Earth, be glad! . . . Light shines on the righteous, and gladness on the good." The beauty of Christ's birth is for the whole earth. The scene showing the birth of the baby Jesus can be just Mary, Joseph, and the baby *(show those three)*. Or it can include the shepherds *(add them)*. Or it can include the Wise Men *(add them)*. And it can expand on and on around the world and through all time.

You and I are a part of the birth of Christ. He came to be our Savior. His light shines on us and gives us his righteousness. We are filled with joy and gladness today because he is our Savior. The earth rejoices today because Christ is here.

God Won't Let You Forget

THE WORD
    The Lord does not let us forget his wonderful actions;
    he is kind and merciful.
                · Psalm 111:4 (First Sunday after Christmas)

THE WORLD
    Five thank-you notes with space for written message

The mailcarrier brought several nice presents to Danille for Christmas. One came from her grandmother who lives in *(name a distant state)*. Another came from her godparents who live in *(another distant place)*. Another present came from her aunt and uncle who live in *(another distant place)*. Danille enjoyed each of the presents even though she did not get to see the people who gave them to her. She could not tell the mailcarrier thank you for the present because she only delivered them.

Danille's mother told her she was old enough to write her own thank-you letters. Danille said she would send thank-you notes to those who gave her gifts, but first she wanted to play with her new toys. Then she went to visit some of her friends to see what they got for Christmas. She forgot to write the thank-you notes.

The next morning when Danille ate breakfast she found this *(show a thank-you note)* by her plate. Do you know what this is? See, it says "Thank You" on the outside. But the inside is blank. What do you think belongs in that blank space? That's where you are to write a message to say you appreciate the gift.

Why do you think Danille's mother put the note by the plate?

Danille was busy that day too and didn't write any letters. The next day she found another blank note by her plate, and the next day another one. Each morning Danille's mother gave her a note like this until Danille remembered to write her letters to say thanks for the gifts.

God has also given you a gift for Christmas. He does not want you to forget the gift. Listen to what Psalm 111 says, "The Lord does not let us forget his wonderful actions; he is kind and merciful." Danille's mother did not let her forget the gifts she had received. By giving her daughter another gift, like this *(show the notes)*, each day, the mother kept reminding her of the gifts she had received for Christmas.

God also keeps reminding you of the gift he gave you on Christmas by giving you more gifts. First God gave you Jesus to be with you. Then Jesus became the one who died on the cross to pay for your sins—that's another gift from God. Then Jesus rose from the dead so he can still be with you—that's another gift. Today he is kind to you when he speaks to you and hears your prayers—that's another gift. Today he is merciful to you when he forgives your sins—that's another gift.

God won't let you forget that he loves you. I want to remind you to be thankful to God. Saying thank you to God is more than being polite. When you say thank you to God you are showing you believe in him. Your thankfulness shows you love him. But above all you need to thank God every day because he gives you his love every day. God won't let you forget that he loves you.

What Is Most Valuable?

THE WORD

When I look at the sky, which you have made,
at the moon and the stars, which you set in their places
—what is man, that you think of him;
mere man, that you care for him?
Yet you made him inferior only to yourself;
you crowned him with glory and honor
                    Psalm 8:3-5 (The Name of Jesus)

THE WORLD

A piece of good jewelry and a rare book

Adam, would you please hold this jewelry? Take good care of it because it is valuable. That is a real diamond *(or pearls, gold, etc.)*. Would you also hold this book? Don't drop it or tear it, because it is old and cannot be replaced. Both of these things are valuable.

I would like for the rest of you to decide which of these three things is the most valuable. You know that jewelry can cost a lot of money. You may know that old books can be expensive. But before you decide which costs the most, remember I said to look at three things. The first is the jewelry, the second is the book; what do you think the third is? It's Adam, who is holding the other two. We could put a price tag on the other two. They might be expensive. But we couldn't put a price tag on a person. A person is more valuable than money or the things that money can buy.

We live with so many people that we sometimes forget how valuable they are. Listen to what Psalm 8 says, "When I look at the sky, which you have made, at the moon and the stars, which you set in their places—what is man, that you think of him; mere man, that you care for him? Yet you made him inferior only to yourself; you crowned him with glory and honor."

God made many beautiful and wonderful things. The psalm mentions the sky, the moon, and the stars. God also made the flowers, the oceans, and the mountains. He made diamonds and other jewels. But none of God's creation is as important to him as people. God made people to be second only to himself. He loves us so much he sent his Son to become a person with us. We have just celebrated Christmas—the story of Jesus' birth. Jesus is God who became a person.

Jesus became the most important person who ever lived. He is important because he is God who became a human being. He is important because he died to pay for our sins and yet he still lives as our Savior. The great thing about Jesus is that he did not keep his importance for himself. He gave his life for us. Adam is worth more than all the jewelry and books in the world because God loves him. The Father created him. Jesus died for him.

You are important too. You are God's child. As you begin this new year, look at all the wonderful things we have in the world. Then look at yourself and other people. People are the most important part of your life. Enjoy other people and let other people enjoy you.

The Lord Takes—The Lord Gives

THE WORD

> He [the Lord] sends hail like gravel;
> no one can endure the cold he sends!
> Then he gives a command, and the ice melts;
> he sends the wind, and the water flows.
>> Psalm 147:17-18 (Second Sunday after Christmas)

THE WORLD

The words *"Big Joy"* printed on one piece of paper and *"Big Problems"* on another and a clothespin

---

Can you read this? It says, "Big Problems." Maybe you have had a big problem sometime. You might have one now. What are some of the big problems that bother you and your family? *(Talk about sickness, bad weather, worries about jobs, accidents, etc. Include recent events in your congregation or community.)*

Can you read this? It says, "Big Joy." You also have had happy things in your life. I hope you are happy now. What are some of the things that make you happy? We have just celebrated Christmas. We are happy because Jesus came to be our Savior. *(Talk about other happy things: family being together, gifts, good weather, etc. Mention local events.)*

We have both big problems and big joys in our lives. Which ones will last longer, the problems or the joys? Job said it this way, "The Lord gave, and now he has taken away. May his name be praised!" (Job 1:21). In Job's life God gave joys. *(Hand the "Big Joy" sign to a child.)* He was happy. Then God took the joy away and gave him big problems. *(Take the first sign away and use the clothespin to fasten the second to the child's back.)* We like to hold big joys where everyone can see them. But big problems always seem like a load on our backs. Job had joys, but he lost them. Then he had problems. But he knew God still loved him and he still loved God. *(Take both signs again.)*

The psalmist saw problems and joys in another way. First he had big problems. He said "[The Lord] sends hail like gravel; no one can endure the cold he sends!" *(Pin the "Big Problems" sign on a child's back.)* Many people know the problem of cold weather this time of the year. We have other problems too. We live in a world that has many problems. We cause some problems for ourselves. Other people cause some problems for us. Some problems are just a part of life in a sinful world.

Jesus also came to live in this world with its problems. He came to help us live with the problems and finally to remove them. First he came to take away our problems. The psalm first describes the problem of cold weather, then it says, "Then [the Lord] gives a command, and the ice melts; he sends the wind, and the water flows." The Lord took the problem of cold away. He gave the joy of good spring weather. Jesus also helps us in our problems. First he helps get rid of the problem. *(Remove the sign from the child's back.)* Then he gives us joy. *(Hand the other sign to the child.)* First he died for our sins to remove the problem of guilt. Then he rose from the dead to give us eternal life.

Sometimes we see life as Job did. The Lord gives and the Lord takes away. But more often we will see life like this psalm does. The Lord takes away a problem. The Lord gives joy.

A King Like His Father

THE WORD

Teach the king to judge with your righteousness,
O God; share with him your own justice,
so that he will rule over your people with justice
and govern the oppressed with righteousness.

Psalm 72:1-2 (Epiphany)

THE WORLD

A cookie cutter and a variety of cookies, one made
with the cookie cutter

Look at each of these cookies. *(Hold them up one at a time.)* Can you tell which cookie was made with this cookie cutter? First look at the size and shape of the cutter. Then look at all the cookies and find one that is the same size and the same shape. See—this cookie was formed by this cutter. They match.

Today's psalm is a prayer for a king who will match God. Think about all the kings and rulers, there are now and have been in the past in the world. There are a lot more kings and rulers than I have cookies here. Do you think any of the leaders could be like God? The psalm asks for one when it says, "Teach the king to judge with your righteousness, O God; share with him your own justice, so that he will rule over your people with justice and govern the oppressed with righteousness."

God is righteous and fair. He loves people, not just the people of one nation. He wants all people to be treated equally. He wants to help all people who are in need. The psalm prays, "Let's have a king that is like God." Just as a cookie cutter makes a cookie like itself, we ask God to make a king for us who is like himself.

God answered this prayer when Jesus was born. Jesus is like God because he is God's Son. Just as God loves all people, Jesus loves all people. Like God, Jesus judges people fairly. Like God, Jesus wants to help all people in need.

Jesus came to earth to be a king. Just as I have many cookies here and only one came from this cookie cutter, there are many rulers and kings in the world, but only one came to rule over all people with God's justice. That one is Jesus.

Jesus was born in a stable in a small town. His parents were not important to the people of that day. Yet Wise Men from a faraway land came to worship Jesus and to give him gifts. Already at his birth some people knew that the baby would become a king.

Jesus showed the world he was a king when he showed us he was his Father's Son. Because he wanted to help all people in need, he died on a cross to pay for all the sins of all people. Because he wanted to rule with justice like his Father, he rose from the dead to give us victory over sin and death. Jesus is a king like his Father.

Know a King When You See One

THE WORD

That is why God, your God, has chosen you
and has poured out more happiness on you
than on any other king.
The perfume of myrrh and aloes is on your clothes;
musicians entertain you in palaces decorated with ivory.
Psalm 45:7-8 (First Sunday after the Epiphany)

THE WORLD

Firefighter's hat and nurse's cap or other items of
clothing that indicate a person's job. If you are a pastor,
use vestments.

If you saw someone wearing this hat, would you know what the person did? Sure, this hat belongs to a firefighter. You recognize a nurse because nurses wear this type of cap. You can tell I am a pastor because I have on these vestments. Many people wear uniforms that show what work they do.

The psalm for today tells us how to recognize a king. It says, "That is why God, your God, has chosen you and has poured out more happiness on you than on any other king. The perfume of myrrh and aloes is on your clothes; musicians entertain you in palaces decorated with ivory." The king had perfume on his clothing. You could tell he was king because he smelled good. He had a palace with expensive furniture and his own musicians. You could tell he was a king because he lived in a beautiful house.

We can still recognize rulers because they have expensive clothing and beautiful houses. I suppose they also smell good, but we probably don't get close enough to notice. Many rulers and rich people have such things. But I want to help you recognize a special king. He is different than the other kings. He was born in a stable, not a palace. When he was born people gave him gifts, including myrrh, a perfume that smells good. But we don't know that he ever wore the perfume on his clothing.

This king didn't live in a palace. Those who live in palaces have servants who take care of them. Instead this king went out to be a servant for others and to take care of them.

This special king finally got a crown. But it was not made of gold and jewels like the crowns of other kings. His crown was made of thorns.

You know I am talking about the king whose name is Jesus. The story about Jesus is sad because Jesus was always with people who had problems. It is sad because Jesus himself suffered and died on a cross. One of the ways we recognize Jesus is by his suffering. We know he is a king because he loves people. Jesus is a king today, and he still wants to help people.

However, Jesus is a happy king. He is happy, not because he smelled good or lived in a palace, but because his suffering paid off. Yes, because he loved us he had to die. But he came back to life again. We can recognize Jesus as our king now because he gives us victory over sin and death.

Listen to the stories in the Bible about Jesus. Learn what he did and what he said. Then you will be able to recognize him in the world today. You will not see him in a palace. You won't smell his clothing. But you will see his love in the people who live with him. You will receive his help through the people he has helped. And you will know he is your king.

Bless Me So That...

God, be merciful to us and bless us; look on us with kindness, so that the whole world may know your will; so that all nations may know your salvation.

Psalm 67:1-2 (Second Sunday after the Epiphany)

THE WORLD

An expensive doll and a basketball

Shortly before her birthday, Tina and her family moved. Tina didn't know anyone near her new home. She was lonely. On her birthday her parents took her shopping with them. Then told her she could pick out her own present. At first Tina looked at this *(show the doll)*. Her parents knew she liked dolls. They thought she would want it.

Suddenly Tina walked to a different part of the store. She picked up this *(show the basketball)* and said, "I want this for my birthday." Her parents were surprised. They knew Tina liked basketball, But they thought she'd rather have the doll.

On the way home Tina's father asked her why she chose the basketball. She said, "I liked the doll. But I would have played with the doll by myself. If I take the basketball to the park, others will play with it too." The doll would have been for Tina alone. The basketball was for her, but others would enjoy it with her.

When you pray, God lets you choose what you ask for. You may ask God to give you things for yourself. Listen to the prayer of the Jewish people in Psalm 67, "God be merciful to us and bless us; look on us with kindness." We understand that prayer; we also pray that way. We say, "God, be good to us. Take care of us. Love us."

But that wasn't the end of the prayer. They also included two reasons why God should give them what they asked for. They said, ". . . so that the whole world may know your will; so that all nations may know your salvation." The people told God, "Bless us so that other nations may be blessed too." They were like Tina. They didn't want a gift only for themselves. She wanted the basketball so others could play with her. The Jewish people wanted a blessing from God so they could share the blessing with other nations.

We can pray the same way. When you ask God for something, add the words "so that . . . ," then tell God why you want the gift. It's OK for you to ask God to give you things for yourself. But sometimes we want things so that we will have more than others. Sometimes we want things that would separate us from others. Instead we can ask God to bless us so that we will have ways to bless others.

Think about the most important gift of all. God gave his Son Jesus to be your Savior. Because Jesus died for you, your sins are forgiven. Because Jesus is alive again, you have a new life that will last forever. Now add the words "so that . . ." to the gift God gave you in Jesus. God forgave your sins so that you can forgive others. God gave you a new life so that you can tell others that Jesus offers them the same gift.

Now think about all the other things you pray for. Ask God to bless you in many ways so that you will be able to be a blessing for others.

Can You See What God Says?

THE WORD

More than once I have heard God say
that power belongs to him
and that his love is constant.
>   Psalm 62:11-12a (Third Sunday after the Epiphany)

THE WORLD

Motions used to show the children what to do

(Do not say anything as the sermon starts. Greet the children by waving. Put your forefinger in front of your lips to tell the children to be quiet. Use your hands to motion for the children to stand. Motion for them to take several steps toward you. Point to a cross. Motion for them to return to their places and to sit down.)

Did you hear what I told you to do? Each of you did all the things I wanted you to do. That means you received a message from me. But I didn't say a word. You saw what I wanted you to do because you watched my motions. Yet, in one way, you could say you heard what I had to say. You heard the message by what you saw rather than what you listened to.

In the psalm for today King David says, "More than once I have heard God say that power belongs to him and that his love is contsant." David says he heard God. When we read the story of David's life, we find out how he heard God. He heard God because prophets spoke to him. He also heard God because he saw God involved in his life. He heard God say he was powerful when God helped him kill a lion and win battles against his enemies. He heard God say his love was constant when he saw God still loved him and forgave him even when he had done wrong things.

How do you hear what God says? Some of you are old enough to read the Bible and Bible stories. All of you are here to listen to what I say and you know I will give you a message from God through the Scripture. You can hear God's words with your ears. But you can also see what God has to say to you. Remember how you understood the motions I made? You can also understand God's motions when you know God is involved in your life. Like David you can hear God tell you that he has power. You can see his power in the sunshine and the rain. You can see his power in the great things he has made. *(Mention special things of creation in your area: mountains, oceans, rivers, fields that produce food, mines, trees, etc.)*

You can also see God tell you that his love is constant. With your ears you hear the story of Jesus. You hear that Jesus loves you so much he died to pay for your sins and to give you a life that will never end. You hear that even though he died, he came back to life again and still lives with you. You can hear that story with your ears, but you can also see it with your eyes. When you see people who love you and want you to know about Jesus, you see his love in action. When you see people who are forgiven and who forgive you, you see his love.

Other people will also see what God says through you. When you love others, they will see God's love. When you forgive others, they will see God's forgiveness. Listen to God's Word with your ears, but also use your eyes to see his power and love.

Make Sure You're Plugged In

THE WORD

Instead, they find joy in obeying the Law of the Lord,
and they study it day and night.
They are like trees that grow beside a stream,
that bear fruit at the right time,
and whose leaves do not dry up.
           Psalm 1:2-3a (Fourth Sunday after the Epiphany)

THE WORLD

Two electric lamps—one plugged in and one not

You probably have lamps that look something like these in your home. Why do you have lamps? They look nice. Maybe your family bought some lamps to match other things in your house. But we have lamps for a more important reason—to make light.

So, let's have light. *(Turn on the one that is plugged in.)* There is light. *(Turn the switch on the second.)* There is no light from this one. See, it also has a bulb. *(Turn the switch several times.)* Do you know why this light works, and this one does not? *(Let the children discover that one is not plugged in. Plug the second one in and turn it on.)*

You already know that lamps have to be plugged in in order for them to make light. Do you know that you also need to be plugged in to a source of power in order for you to do what God wants to help you do? Listen to part of Psalm 1. It says, "They find joy in obeying the Law of the Lord, and they study it day and night. They are like trees that grow beside a stream, that bear fruit at the right time, and whose leaves do not dry up."

The psalm says that people who study God's Word are like trees near a stream of water. Trees that have water grow and produce fruit. Trees that do not have water cannot grow or produce fruit. They will die without water. Trees need water just like these lamps need electricity.

People also need a source of power. We need food to make our bodies grow. Without food we would not be healthy and would soon die. But we need more than food. We also need power for our spiritual lives. God gives us that power through Jesus Christ.

We connect to God's power in Christ when we read and hear his Word. In the Bible he tells us that Jesus came to live with us. We learn that Jesus helped people. Sometimes he helped one person who was sick by making that person well. Then he helped all people by dying on the cross to forgive everyone's sin. He rose from the dead. He came back to be with us in a special way.

When you hear the gospel, the good news that Jesus is your Savior, you are like a tree growing near a river or like a lamp that is plugged into an electrical outlet. You receive power from God. You know God loves you. You know you are forgiven. You know he helps you.

All of us have times when we feel we run out of power. We feel as though our lights won't go on. When that happens, remember where your power comes from. Make sure you're plugged in to the message from God. Listen to the story of Jesus. He gives you the power to light up your life.

What Makes God Happy?

THE WORD

[God's] pleasure is not in strong horses,
nor his delight in brave soldiers;
but he takes pleasure in those who honor him,
in those who trust in his constant love.

Psalm 147:10-11 (Fifth Sunday after the Epiphany)

THE WORLD

A child's book, a game, and a stuffed toy

A woman who had no children kept these three things in her home. When children came to visit, she put these things out for them to play with. The woman learned something about the children who visited her. She could tell what made them happy by seeing which of the things each one chose. Some liked to read. Others like to play games. Others liked the stuffed toy. Which one of these would make you happy?

Now let's imagine that God is coming to visit the earth. I know God is here all the time, but let's think of him as coming for a special visit. Of all the wonderful things on the earth, which ones would make God happy? What would he want to see first? Would he stop to see the mountains and oceans? Would he want to see a big city? Would he want to be with the army that wins wars, or the football team that wins all the games?

Listen to what the psalm for today tells us. It says, "[God's] pleasure is not in strong horses, nor his delight in brave soldiers." Horses were the strong animals of that day. Soldiers won wars and made nations strong. But those were not the things that made God happy. He is not impressed with power and strength because he has more power than all the horses and soldiers put together.

First the psalm told us what God does not find his pleasure in. Now it tells us what does make God happy. It says, "But he takes pleasure in those who honor him, in those who trust in his constant love." God is happy to be with those who know him and respect him. He is happy to be with those who love him.

This means you don't have to show off to impress God. You don't have to have beautiful clothes or an expensive home. You don't have to get good grades or be on the winning team to make God enjoy being with you.

God already loves you and wants to be with you. Jesus is God who became a human being to live with us. But when Jesus came to live on this earth many people hated him and caused him to be killed. But Jesus still loved all people. He let them kill him because he knew he had to die to pay for all the sins of the world. By his death and his rising from the dead, he showed his great love for all people.

God still wants to be with us. We are here now to worship him. We are happy to be with him because we love him. We show we care about him because we decided to come and worship him. God is happy to be with us because we are here to honor him and we trust in his love.

Don't Hide the Pain

THE WORD

When I did not confess my sins,
I was worn out from crying all day long.
Day and night you punished me, Lord;
my strength was completely drained,
as moisture is dried up by the summer heat.
Then I confessed my sins to you;
I did not conceal my wrongdoings.
I decided to confess them to you,
and you forgave all my sins.
                    Psalm 32:3-5 (Sixth Sunday after the Epiphany)

THE WORLD

A small rock with sharp edges

I want to show you something that might be hard to see from a distance. See this rock? It's small with sharp edges. I picked a small rock because I want to hide it. May I hide it in your shoe, Tina? *(Put the rock in a child's shoe. Hold her hand so she will walk with you.)* Can any of you see the rock? It is well hidden.

Can you see the rock, Tina? You can't see it, but you know where it is because you can feel it. How does it feel when you walk with a rock in your shoe? Would you like to keep the rock there the rest of the day?

When you hide the rock in your shoe, it hurts your foot. In the psalm for today King David tries to hide something, and it hurts him too. Listen to what he wrote: "When I did not confess my sins, I was worn out from crying all day long. Day and night you punished me, Lord; my strength was completely drained, as moisture is dried up by the summer heat."

David hid his sin. He had done bad things, but he pretended to be good. Other people could not see his sin, just as the rest of us can't see the rock in Tina's shoe. But David could feel his sin. It hurt him. He cried. He felt weak. He felt burned out.

David couldn't stand the pain any more. Listen to what he did: "Then I confessed my sins to you; I did not conceal my wrongdoings. I decided to confess them to you, and you forgave all my sins." David asked God to forgive him. God took away the pain of his sin. He was free again.

If Tina takes the rock out of her shoe, it won't hurt anymore. But if she keeps on hiding the rock there, she will hurt. Sin in our hearts is like rocks in our shoes. They hurt. No one can see them, but we can feel the pain. But Jesus can see the sin. He can also feel the pain. He felt the pain for us. That's why he suffered and died to pay for our sins. He took away the pain of our sins when he was nailed to the cross and died for us.

Don't hide your sins from God. You can do what David did. Confess your sins. Show your sins to God. He loves you. He forgives you. He takes away your sins and you don't have to hurt any more.

Learn How to Give

THE WORD

Happy are those who are concerned for the poor;
the Lord will help them when they are in trouble.
The Lord will protect them and preserve their lives;
he will make them happy in the land.
Psalm 41:1-2a (Seventh Sunday after the Epiphany)

THE WORLD

Two apples (or other fresh fruit)

When Donna and Beth's grandparents came to visit, they brought a whole basket of apples. The family enjoyed the apples, but it was a big basket, so they had more than they could eat. One day when the girls' mother was packing their snack for school she put in an apple for each of them, then she added these two extra apples *(show apples)*. Their mother said, "I am sending an extra apple with each of you. You may give it to someone at school."

On the way to school Donna thought about giving the apple away. Who would she give it to? There was a rich girl in Donna's class and Donna wanted to go to her house. She thought to herself, "If I give the apple to the rich girl, she will know that I like her. Then maybe she will invite me to her house."

Beth also thought about giving her apple way. She remembered a girl in her class who was poor. The poor girl never brought any snacks to school. Beth decided to give the apple to the poor girl.

When Donna gave the apple to the rich girl, the girl accepted it and put it in her desk. She already had lots of fresh fruit at home. Several days later

38

Donna noticed the apple was still in the rich girl's desk. It had a bad spot and wouldn't be good to eat any more.

When Beth gave her apple to the poor girl, the other girl was glad to get it. She said thank you several times, and she and Beth ate their apples together. They became friends.

I told you the story about Donna, Beth, and the apples to help you learn how to give. The psalm for today gives us a lesson about giving when it says, "Happy are those who are concerned for the poor; the Lord will help them when they are in trouble. The Lord will protect them and preserve their lives; he will make them happy in the land."

The psalm was written by a rich man, King David. But he tells us to be concerned about the poor. Donna did not know how to care about anyone else. She did not give the apple away to help someone. She gave the apple away to help herself. The rich girl did not need or appreciate the apple. Beth gave her apple to someone who needed it. The poor girl was glad to get the apple. She also was glad to have Beth as a friend.

Jesus knew how to give. He gave himself to be our Savior. Jesus loves us. He died on the cross to pay for our sins and give us eternal life. Jesus showed us how to receive a gift from him—and how to give gifts to others. We can see what others need. We can give to them. We give to them when we tell them about Jesus. We give to them when we help them just as Jesus helped people who were in need. God promises us that if we care about people who are poor he will take care of us. When we learn to give to others we also understand how much God has given to us.

Don't Forget
What You Already Have

THE WORD

Praise the Lord, my soul,
and do not forget how kind he is.
He forgives all my sins and heals all my diseases.
He keeps me from the grave and blesses me with
love and mercy.
He fills my life with good things.
  Psalm 103:2-5a (Eighth Sunday after the Epiphany)

THE WORLD

A pocketknife with various accessories including a
screwdriver and can opener. Boy Scouts often have
such knives.

Adam bought this pocketknife *(show the knife)*
when he joined the Boy Scouts. He needed it for
camping trips, but he liked to keep it with him all
the time. One day he was with his father when they
had car trouble. The father tried to fix the car, but he
needed a screwdriver. Since they didn't have one,
Adam and his father had to walk home. Another time
the family was on a picnic. They had brought food in
cans, but they had no can opener. They could not use
that food.

Later when Adam was on a camping trip he used
his pocketknife. When he opened the knife he remembered that one of the blades was a screwdriver. *(Show
it.)* His father could have used that to fix the car.
Another blade was a can opener. *(Show it.)* They
could have opened the cans on the picnic. Adam had
the tools they needed, but he forgot to use them.

The psalm for today says we might forget to use
all the gifts God gives us. First it says, "Praise the

Lord, my soul, and do not forget how kind he is."
We often praise God because he created us. That is
good. But he also offers much more. Just as Adam's
pocketknife had blades like a knife and also other
tools, God has many ways to help us. The psalm tells
us not to forget all the kind things God does.

The psalm lists some of the things God does that
we might forget. It says, "[God] forgives all my sins
and heals all my diseases. He keeps me from the grave
and blesses me with love and mercy. He fills my life
with good things." We could add even more to the
list of the kind things God does, but first let's remember these.

God forgives our sins. The greatest thing Jesus did
for us was to die to pay for the wrongs we have done.
He has taken away our guilt. Let's not forget to use his
forgiveness when we need it.

When Jesus forgives us he takes away our spiritual
sickness. He also heals our bodies. When we are sick,
we ask him to make us well. When we are well we
ask him to keep us in good health. Let's not forget to
ask him to take care of us.

Jesus also keeps us from the grave. He protects us
from accidents and other things that could kill us.
Even when we die, he promises that he will bring us
back out of our graves just as he came out of his
grave. Let's not forget that.

The psalm says, "He fills my life with good things."
Remember the good things God has given you. Your
family and friends. Games you like to play. Places you
like to go. Don't forget what God has given you.

Sometimes we are like Adam who forgot all the
ways he could use his pocketknife. We forget to use
all the blessings that God offers us. The best way to
remember is to think often about Jesus and see how
much he loves you. Then you can remember all the
ways he helps you.

A Light That Shines Everywhere

THE WORD

The Almighty God, the Lord, speaks;
he calls to the whole earth from east to west.
God shines from Zion,
the city perfect in its beauty.

> Psalm 50:1-2 (The Transfiguration of our Lord)

THE WORLD

A small flashlight and the lights in your building

The psalm for today tells us, "God shines from Zion, the city perfect in its beauty." Zion is the name for the city of God. Think of God shining on a city and making it bright. Remember what happened when Jesus was up on a mountain with three of his disciples? The disciples saw Jesus change before their eyes. Before he had looked like other people. Then he became shining white. They saw Jesus as the psalm for today describes him.

Think of this flashlight *(show it)* as Jesus. See, it also shines. I can shine it on you, on you, and on you. When Jesus shines his light on you, think of it as his love. When the light shines on you, it means Jesus died for you to take away your sin. It means he rose from the dead and lives with you now. It means he is the light of your world and he leads you from here to heaven.

Isn't it nice to think of this light as Christ shining on you? But there is a problem. When it shines on you, it does not shine on all those other people. Instead of thinking of this flashlight as being Jesus, let's think of the lights in the church as being the light of

Christ. Look at those lights *(point to the lights)*. When they shine on you, they also shine on others. When they shine on these people here, they also shine on those over there. This means Jesus died for everyone who is here. This means he loves all of us. Isn't that good to hear?

Now we have another problem. The church lights shine only in this building. We don't stay in here all the time. There are many people in other churches or in no church at all. Jesus also loves them. Listen to something else the psalm says, "The Almighty God, the Lord, speaks; he calls to the whole earth from east to west."

When God speaks he does not speak just to you and me. God is not like this flashlight that shines on one or two people at a time. He does not speak only to those in this building. He is not like our lights that shine only here. God speaks his message of love to all people. Let's look for another light that reminds us that God loves all people.

What about the light that comes up every morning in the east and goes down every evening in the west? The sun is a better example of God who shines from Zion. The sun shines on all people. God loves all people. The sun can remind us that Jesus died for everyone. It reminds us that he invites all people to believe in him.

It's OK to Cry

THE WORD
> I can hardly see; my eyes are so swollen
> from the weeping caused by my enemies.
> Keep away from me, you evil men!
> The Lord hears my weeping;
> he listens to my cry for help
> and will answer my prayer.
>
> Psalm 6:7-9 (First Sunday in Lent)

THE WORLD
A box of tissues

===

One of the nice things about being a child is that you can cry when you feel like it. Sometimes adults feel that they shouldn't cry. I want to tell you today that it is OK to cry—even after you become an adult.

David was the great king of Israel. He was a hero. He also knew how to cry. Listen to what he said in Psalm 6: "I can hardly see; my eyes are so swollen from the weeping caused by my enemies. Keep away from me, you evil men! The Lord heard my weeping; he listens to my cry for help."

David cried because his enemies hurt him. His enemies killed some of his friends, so he cried. His enemies took things David owned away from him, so he cried. His enemies worried him, so he cried. His enemies made him angry, so he cried. His enemies may have even cut him with a sword or spear and it hurt, so he cried.

We are like King David. We get hurt, worried, disappointed, angry. So we cry. It is not wrong for us to cry. Crying does not solve our problems, yet we feel better after we cry. Our tears help us face our problems. Our tears show that we do not have to pretend everything is OK. Our tears let us admit we are sad.

But our tears also do something else to help us. Our tears show others that we need help. When you cry your parents, teachers, and friends know you need help. They come with a tissue *(show the box and pull out a tissue)* to wipe away the tears. As they help wipe away the tears they listen to what the problem is.

God also listens when you cry. David said, "The Lord hears my weeping; he listens to my cry for help." Think of your crying as a prayer. God hears your need. He comes to wipe away your tears and to listen to your problems.

When Jesus lived on earth he felt pain and sorrow. He cried. He cried because he felt the pains we feel. But Jesus did more than just cry about our problems. He also did something to help us. He died to take away the sin that hurts us. He rose from the dead to show us that even death will not destroy us or our family and friends. Because Jesus is our Savior we will live together with him in heaven.

I want to give each of you a tissue as you leave today. *(Give out tissues as you talk.)* I give you these tissues because I know you will have to cry sometime. Because you are a Christian does not mean you will not have problems. It does mean Jesus will be with you to help you. He will hear your cries as though they were prayers. When you use a tissue to wipe away your tears, remember Jesus is with you. He cried too. He helps you.

Who Gets the Glory?

THE WORD

To you alone, O Lord, to you alone,
and not to us, must glory be given
because of your constant love and faithfulness.

Psalm 115:1 (Second Sunday in Lent)

THE WORLD

A jigsaw puzzle (for the age of children present) put
together except for the final piece. Fasten the puzzle
to a board so it may be shown.

Ryan liked to work jigsaw puzzles. He worked a
long time to put this one together. *(Hold it up.)* See,
it is all done except for one piece. Just as he was
about to finish the puzzle, Ryan got a phone call.
While he was gone his brother Shawn came along.
He picked up the last piece of the puzzle and put
it in place.

That night at dinner, Shawn said, "Look at the
puzzle I put together." The boys' parents said, "That
is good, Shawn. You did a fine job. We know you
worked hard." How do you think Ryan felt? Shawn
did put the last piece of the puzzle in place, but that
was the easy one. Anyone could find the place for the
last piece of a puzzle. Ryan did all the work, but
Shawn took the credit for doing it.

Think about that story as you listen to the first
verse of Psalm 115. "To you alone, O Lord, to you
alone, and not to us, must glory be given because of
your constant love and faithfulness."

The psalm writer knew that we sometimes do to
God what Shawn did to Ryan. We let God do the

work, and we try to take the credit. God gives us healthy bodies and minds so we can do wonderful things. Then we think we are great because we can play or work well. God gives us a beautiful world full of many wonderful things. Instead of thanking him for what he has given us, we sometimes take credit for what he has done. But this psalm reminds us that God alone should have the glory and the thanks for what he has done.

Think about what Jesus has done for you. He could have stayed in heaven. Instead he came to live on this earth. He had to see sin and even be tempted to join in the sins of the world. People laughed at him. They hit him. His friends ran away and hid. They left him all alone. Finally, soldiers nailed him to a cross and he died.

Do you know why Jesus did all of that? The one who wrote Psalm 115 tells us it was because of God's constant love and faithfulness. Jesus suffered and died because he loves us. He took punishment for sin that should have been given to us. He died for us because he could win a victory over death by coming back to life. Now when we die, we know that because of Jesus we will come back to life and go to heaven.

Sometimes people say they are going to heaven because they go to church, or because they say their prayers, or because they do good. That is like Shawn saying he put the puzzle together when Ryan did all the work. Jesus has done the work for us. We are going to heaven because he saved us. We can say what the psalmist said, "To you alone, O Lord, to you alone, and not to us, must glory be given because of your constant love and faithfulness."

How to Be Acceptable

THE WORD
May my words and my thoughts be acceptable to you,
O Lord, my refuge and my redeemer!
                    Psalm 19:14 (Third Sunday in Lent)

THE WORLD
Two pieces of bread, a piece of cheese, and a piece of
cardboard

Today I'd like to talk to you about one word. The word is *acceptable*. Listen to what King David said in Psalm 19, "May my words and my thoughts be acceptable to you, O Lord, my refuge and my redeemer."

Do you know what *acceptable* means? It means "I can use that." It means "That's fine with me." Let me give you an example of acceptable. Suppose you are hungry and ask me for something to eat. I tell you I will give you a sandwich. That is acceptable. A sandwich is what you need when you are hungry. So I take these two pieces of bread *(show them)* and place a piece of cardboard between them. This is a cardboard sandwich *(show it)*. That would not be acceptable to you. However, if I take out the cardboard and put the cheese in, it is acceptable *(show cheese sandwich)*. Then you could eat it.

Now let's think about what King David said. He wanted his words and his thoughts to be acceptable to God. We want the same thing. Think about all the things you said last week. Pretend all of your words were recorded on a tape. You know that some of the things you said would be acceptable to God. He heard your prayers. That means he accepted them.

48

He heard the polite and good things you said to your parents, friends, and teachers. Those words were acceptable to God.

But do you think all of your words were acceptable to God? Do you think he could say, "That's fine, I can use that," to everything you said?

Remember, David also wants God to accept his thoughts. Pretend everything that you thought was on a tape. Many of your prayers are thoughts rather than words. God accepted them. But you may also have thought angry and bad things. You may have thought things that you would not even have said to anyone. Would God accept them?

When David asks God to accept his words and thoughts, he is not asking God to lower his standards. He does not want God to enjoy bad words and thoughts any more than I would expect you to eat a cardboard sandwich. Instead David asks God to make his words and thoughts acceptable. He knows he has said and thought bad things. But he also knows God is his refuge, that is, his safe place. He knows God is his redeemer, the one who makes him acceptable.

I made the cardboard sandwich acceptable to you by taking out the cardboard and putting in a piece of cheese. God also makes your words and thoughts acceptable by taking out the bad things and putting in his good. Jesus is your Savior. When he died to pay for your sins, he took the guilt out of your words and thoughts. When he rose from the dead, he gave you a new life. In Christ, your words and thoughts are acceptable to God.

Listen to your own words and thoughts. When you think they are not acceptable to God, do what David did. Ask God to make your words and thoughts acceptable to him. He is your safe place. He is your redeemer. He will help you.

Come to Me

THE WORD

When you said, "Come worship me,"
I answered, "I will come, Lord."
Don't hide yourself from me!

Psalm 27:8-9a (Fourth Sunday in Lent)

THE WORLD

A blindfold

Jenny, I need you to help me. Will you come here and touch my hand? *(Move to another place.)* Will you come here? See, it is easy for you to come to me as long as you can see me.

May I put this blindfold on you, Jenny? I will be near so you will not be hurt. I want the others to see what you will feel. Now that you cannot see me, you cannot come to me. *(If the child is old enough, and if you are using a sound system, go to a distant microphone and ask the child to come to you. Explain the frustration of hearing the voice come from various speakers. It confuses the child so she does not know which way to go. Then continue as follows.)*

Can you come to me now, Jenny? *(Help her follow your voice to you.)* Even though she cannot see me she can come to where I am. Let's try it again. *(Move to another place.)* Jenny, come here. Touch my hand. See, she can do it. *(Take off the blindfold and thank her.)*

When Jesus lived on earth the disciples could follow him just as Jenny could follow me before I put the blindfold on her. When Jesus walked to Jerusalem they followed him because they saw him. We think the disciples had it easy. They could see Jesus and follow him.

But we can't see Jesus. It is more difficult for us to be with him. King David lived long before Jesus was born, so he could not see him either. Yet listen to what David wrote: "When you said, 'Come worship me,' I answered 'I will come, Lord.' Don't hide yourself from me." David knew God asked him to come worship him. But David could not see God. However, he heard his voice. He read the sacred writings and through them heard God speak to him. He saw how God helped him when he had problems and he knew God was there. So David could go to God and worship him. He did not go to God because he had seen him, but because he had heard him.

If I asked you to go to God, where would you go? You can't see him. Yet you can hear him. In the Bible he tells you to come and worship him just as he told David to come and worship him. When you come to church you do not see God, but you hear his word. You hear the story about Jesus. You know he is the Savior who died to pay for your sins. You know he is still with you because he rose from the dead. You know he will be with you forever.

I asked Jenny to wear the blindfold to show you she could come to me even if she couldn't see me. She could hear the words I spoke and come to me. You can also hear the words of Jesus and come to him. He not only invites you to come and worship him in church, he also tells you to go out into the world and help people. His words tell you to love one another, to feed hungry people, to help lonely people. When you hear his words you can follow him. You can be with him always because he always speaks to you and you can follow his words.

It's Fun to Be a Christian

THE WORD

Give me again the joy that comes from your salvation,
and make me willing to obey you.
Then I will teach sinners your commands,
and they will turn back to you.

Psalm 51:12-13 (Fifth Sunday in Lent)

THE WORLD

A basketball (or any other sports equipment)

Jimmy liked to play basketball. *(Handle the ball as you talk about it.)* He would get up early in the morning so he could shoot baskets by himself. He would meet friends after school and they would play basketball.

Jimmy became such a good player that he made the school basketball team. Then he had practice every day. He worked hard and was excited about playing against other teams. He didn't like to lose.

But Jimmy found that he wasn't having fun any more. He played games, not because he wanted to, but because he had to. Instead of being excited about a game, he worried because he might make a mistake and cause his team to lose. *(Put the ball away.)*

I told you about Jimmy and basketball because I want to tell you something about your faith in Jesus. We can lose the fun of being a Christian just as Jimmy lost the fun of playing basketball.

It's fun to be a Christian. We know that Jesus loves us. He is our Savior who died to take away our sins. He is our Savior who lives again and is with us. We can wake up every morning and say, "Good morning,

God." We can hear what God says to us by reading and hearing the Bible. We can talk to him when we pray. It is fun to know that Jesus is our friend.

King David had been happy because he knew God. But he got so busy that he forgot about God. He did some wrong things, so he tried to hide from God. Then the king realized he wasn't happy any more. He missed being close to God. So he prayed, "Give me again the joy that comes from your salvation, and make me willing to obey you. Then I will teach sinners your commands, and they will turn back to you." When David realized he wasn't happy any more, he asked for God's help. He wanted to be happy again. He wanted to serve God again. He also said he would teach others. He knew that if he told others about God's love, he would not forget it again.

Are you happy that you are a Christian? Some people lose the joy God gives them. Instead of enjoying God, they think they have to love and serve him. They say, "I have to go to church." "I have to give money." "I have to say my prayers." "If I sin God will be angry with me." They serve God because they think they have to. They don't do it because they want to.

If that happens to you, remember King David. He asked God to give him joy again. You can ask God to give you joy again. You can pray, "God, help me love you. Help me want to serve you. Help me want to hear your word and serve you."

God already loves you. He is happy that you are his. Because Jesus is your Savior you can be with God. It's fun to be a Christian.

Know Where to Go for Help

THE WORD

I come to you, Lord, for protection;
never let me be defeated.
You are a righteous God; save me, I pray! . . .
I place myself in your care.
You will save me, Lord; you are a faithful God.
Psalm 31: 1, 5 (Sunday of the Passion)

THE WORLD

A butterfly net (or other net material), a piece of tissue paper, and an umbrella

---

Suppose you are all dressed and ready to come to church when it starts to rain. You've got to run through the rain to get to the car. Would you put this *(show the net)* over your head? That wouldn't do any good, would it? How about this *(show the tissue paper)*? If you want to keep your head dry, you need something like this *(show the umbrella)*.

When you need help, you need to choose the right kind of help. One time King David had lots of problems. His enemies were attacking him. Even his neighbors were doing bad things to him. He could have said, "I'll use my army to kill all those people." Or he could have said, "I've got lots of money, I'll pay all of them to go away." But he didn't say either of those things. To David that would have been like using a net or tissue paper to protect your head from rain.

David knew where to find help. He said, "I come to you, Lord, for protection; never let me be defeated. You are a righteous God; save me, I pray! . . . I place myself in your care. You will save me, Lord; you are a faithful God."

David did not depend on his army or his money. He depended on God. If I want to keep the rain off, I use an umbrella. When David wanted to be saved from his enemies, he put himself under God's care. God had given David many good things—like health, money, and power. David used those things, but he did not depend on them. Instead, he depended on God who had given him those things.

I told you about King David so you would also know where to get help when you have a problem. God has also given you many good things—things that David didn't have. You are getting a good education. You have doctors and hospitals to help you if you are sick. You live in a free country and are well protected. All of these things are good. But do not depend on them. Instead depend on God who gives those things to you.

David's money and army could have helped him for a while. But sooner or later he had to die like all people. Because he depended on God, he could live and die in peace. God was with him, and David knew it.

God is also with you. He is with you on the good, happy days. He is also with you on the sad, lonely days. Remember what Jesus did for you. He felt pain. He was sad and lonely. He even died for you. When you have pain, when you are sad or lonely, even when you die, Jesus is with you. You can say what David said, "I place myself in your care. You will save me, Lord; you are a faithful God."

How Long Will It Last?

THE WORD

Give thanks to the Lord, because he is good,
and his love is eternal.
Let the people of Israel say,
"His love is eternal."

Psalm 118:1-2 (Easter Sunday)

THE WORLD

Objects available in the church or classroom

Let's play a game called "How long will it last?" I'll point to something and ask you, "How long will it last?" Then you tell me what you think the answer is.

First, the Easter lily. How long do you think it will last? *(Discuss the flowers and buds.)* Next question: How long do you think your clothes will last? *(Talk about how soon the clothes will wear out or the children will outgrow them.)* How long do you think this building will last? *(Talk about the age of the building and compare it to the oldest buildings known by the children.)*

Now, how about you? How long will you last? *(Give the children time to think about the question. If one answers, "Forever," continue from that point.)*

You may live on this earth for 60 or 70 or even more years. But you can last even longer than that. I want to tell you how you can last forever.

Psalm 118 says, "Give thanks to the Lord, because he is good, and his love is eternal. Let the people of Israel say, 'His love is eternal.' " The word *eternal* means without end. Something that is eternal will last forever. The psalm tells us that God's love is eternal.

56

He will always love us. God's love for us will never end.

It is good news to know that God will always love us. But that makes us ask other questions. Can his love for us be eternal if we are not eternal? Could he still love us if we didn't exist any more? How can God's love last forever if we don't?

The answer is that we will also last forever because God's love is eternal. Today we are happy because Jesus rose from the dead. Jesus died, but that was not the end of Jesus. Three days after he died he came back to life again. He died for us because he loved us and wanted to pay for our sins. But that did not end his love. Remember, his love is eternal. So he came back to life to live with us and love us.

Because Jesus rose from the dead, we will also be raised from the dead after we die. His love will last forever and will make us last forever also. Some things will last only a short time—like the Easter lilies. Some things will last for a while longer—like our clothes. Some things will last a long time—like the building. But God's love will last forever, and we will too.

Something for Everyone

THE WORD

Praise him, kings and all peoples,
princes and all other rulers;
girls and young men,
old people and children too.
                    Psalm 148:11-12 (Second Sunday of Easter)

THE WORLD

A baby bottle, a paper cup filled with a fruit drink, and
a cup of coffee—all on a tray

Shelia is thirsty. Would you please get Shelia a drink? So you won't have to go far, I have a tray here. *(Show the tray with the three items on it.)* You may choose one of these things as a drink for Shelia. Which one will you choose?

Before you decide which one to give to Shelia, you need to know how old she is. If Shelia is a baby, you would take this baby bottle to her. If she is a child, you would take her the drink in the paper cup. If she is an adult, you might give her the cup of coffee.

Different people need different things. Children need different things than adults. A poor person would need money. A rich person might need a friend or a time to be alone. There are some things that all people need. We all need food. We all need clothing and a place to live. We all need love.

The psalm for today says we all need to praise God. It says, "Praise him, kings and all peoples, princes and all other rulers; girls and young men, old people and children too." Notice how it lists all people. A poor person can praise God because he sees how great God is. But a king and other rulers can also praise God because God is much greater than they are. Boys, girls, children, old people—everyone can praise God.

We can praise God because God has done great things for all of us. He does not give his help only to one group of people. Think about the things Jesus did. He helped all kinds of people. He gave his love to the rich and the poor, the sick and the healthy, the young and the old, the men and the women.

Jesus loved all people because he knew all people needed him. All of us have sinned. None of us have done all the good that we should do. But Jesus loves us anyway. He died on the cross for all people. For those who have done bad things and are in prison. For those who have done shameful things that no one knows about. For those who have only done things that seem like little sins to us but are all sins against God. Jesus died to forgive them all.

Then Jesus rose from the dead. His victory over death promises that we will live forever. If a king dies, he will be raised from the dead by Jesus. If a poor person dies, Jesus will raise him from the dead. If old people die, if children or babies die, Jesus will raise them all from the dead.

When you praise God you are close to God because you know about his love for you. But when you praise God you are also close to other people. You can praise God because he also loves others. They can praise God because he loves you.

God Already Knows

THE WORD
Lord, you have examined me and you know me.
You know everything I do; from far away
you understand all my thoughts.

Psalm 139:1-2 (Third Sunday of Easter)

THE WORLD

A book (one that can be written on), a pencil, and paper to cover the book

---

Joy's teacher gave her this book *(show book)* when school started. The teacher said the books belonged to the school and the students were to take good care of them. One day Joy had the book on her desk and a pencil in her hand. She drew some pictures on the cover of the book. *(Do it.)* She wrote her name and names of her friends in the book. Then she remembered it was not her book. She was worried. She took this paper and covered the book so no one could see what she had done. *(Do it.)*

Now the teacher could not see the marks that Joy had made on the book. But Joy was still worried. She thought about the end of school. Would the teacher take the cover off the book and see what she had done? Joy worried about what the teacher would say and do.

In one way we are all like Joy. We all want to hide some of the things we have done and said. We would not want our parents to hear everything we have said. We would not want some people to know the things we have done. We would not want anyone to know everything we have thought. Just as Joy used paper to cover the marks on her book, we try to hide the things we have done wrong.

Listen to what today's psalm says: "Lord, you have examined me and you know me. You know everything I do; from far away you understand all my thoughts." God is not like Joy's teacher. He is not like our parents and friends. We cannot hide our sins from him. He knows everything we do. He even knows everything we think.

Does that make you afraid of God? I hope not. I want you to be glad that God knows everything. Remember the story about Joy and her book. She hid the marks she had made. Then she worried about what the teacher would say when she found the marks. If we could hide our sins from God, we would. Then we would worry what God would say when he discovered our sins.

But God already knows. God already knew about our sin when he sent Jesus to be our Savior. Jesus knew about our sin when he said he loved us. He knew about our sin when he died on the cross. In fact, that's why he died for us. He took the punishment for our sins. We don't have to worry about what God will say when he discovers our sin. *(Take the cover off the book.)* He already knows we have sinned. And he has already forgiven our sin.

I am glad God knows all about me. I don't have to be afraid that someday he will find out what I have done wrong and stop loving me. He already knows and he still loves me. He knows everything about you too. He still loves you—and he always will.

Don't Be Afraid of the Dark

THE WORD

Even if I go through the deepest darkness,
I will not be afraid, Lord,
for you are with me.
Your shepherd's rod and staff protect me.

Psalm 23:4 (Fourth Sunday of Easter)

THE WORLD

A blindfold

In the 23rd Psalm King David said, "Even if I go through the deepest darkness, I will not be afraid, Lord, for you are with me. Your shepherd's rod and staff protect me."

You know that a great king like David was not afraid of the dark. He fought against lions and giants. Why should he be afraid of the dark? He tells you why he was not afraid. It was not because he was brave. He was not afraid because God was with him.

By himself David would have been afraid. At night his enemies could sneak up on him and kill him. He would also have been afraid of other kinds of darkness. Looking ahead to tomorrow and next year can seem like looking into darkness because we do not know what will happen. Death can seem like darkness because we cannot see our way through it. But David was not afraid of any kind of darkness because he knew God was with him.

Let's look at darkness. Since we can't make this room totally dark now, I'll put a blindfold on Michele. She is in darkness now, and the rest of you can pretend with her. Michele, go to the altar *(or some place that includes steps).* Michele could easily do that in the light. But in the dark she might trip and fall. Michele, go to where your father is sitting. If she could see that would be easy. But in the dark she might run into something.

Because she is in the dark, Michele is afraid to do even easy things. But I can help her even while she is in the dark. *(Take her hand.)* Now, Michele, let's walk to the altar. See how easy it is when I am with you? I will not let you trip and fall. Let's go to your father. I will not let you bump into anything. *(Remove blindfold from child.)*

When David was in the dark, he knew God was with him. He knew God would lead him safely through the dark places. God is also with you. God sent Jesus to live with us. Jesus walked through the dark places on this earth. He went to where people were in darkness—the darkness of fear and pain. The darkness of sin and death. He helped people in darkness by being with them. He even died to pay for the sins of the world and to let us know he will be with us when we die. He was not afraid of the darkness of death because he knew he would rise from the dead. We need not be afraid of any kind of darkness. Not the darkness of night, not the darkness of what might happen, not even the darkness of death. Jesus is with us and leads us through the darkness.

David's words can also be your words, "Even if I go through the deepest darkness, I will not be afraid, Lord, for you are with me."

Pass It On

THE WORD

Future generations will serve him;
men will speak of the Lord to the coming generation.
People not yet born will be told:
"The Lord saved his people."
Psalm 22:30-31 (Fifth Sunday of Easter)

THE WORLD

An envelope and a piece of paper with the words *"The Lord saved his people"*

There is an important message on this piece of paper. If I wanted someone in *(name another part of the building)* to know the message, what would I do? I could deliver it myself. Or I could ask one of you to take it for me. I could give you the paper and have you deliver it. Or I could tell you the message. It says, "The Lord saved his people." You could remember those words and tell someone else. "The Lord saved his people."

What would I do if I wanted to give the message to someone who lives in Japan? I could take it myself. I could ask someone else to deliver it. But there is an easier way. I could mail it. *(Put the paper in the envelope.)* I could use the mail to send the message anywhere in the world.

What if I wanted to give the message to someone who will live in the year 2000? That is____ years from now. I can't mail the message to someone who will live in the year 2000. But I could tell you the message. Remember, it is, "The Lord saved his people." You could tell the people who will live in the year 2000.

64

What if I wanted to give the message to someone who will live in the year 2100? That is ___ years from now. You can't deliver the message because you won't live that long. I can't mail it to the future. How can I send this message to the people who will live 100 or 200 years from now?

King David lived about 3000 years ago. He knew this message and he knew a way to deliver it to us. Listen to what he said, "Future generations will serve him; men will speak of the Lord to the coming generation. People not yet born will be told: "The Lord saved his people."

David found a way to give his message to people who lived long after him. First, he wrote it down. That's why we can read it today. But that's not all he did. If he had written it and hidden it, we might not have found it today. David told the people he knew that the Lord would save them. They told the people they knew. Parents told their children. The children grew up to be parents who told their children.

Today you know God has saved you. You know Jesus is the Savior who died for your sins. You know he rose from the dead and lives in heaven. You know he will come to take you to heaven. You know these things because they are written in the Bible and because your parents, your teachers, I, and others have given you the message, "The Lord saved his people."

People who will live in the year 2000 and 2100 will also know the message. They will know it because you have heard it and because you pass it on to them through your children and your grandchildren.

Look What You Won!

THE WORD
Sing a new song to the Lord;
he has done wonderful things!
By his own power and holy strength
he has won the victory.
The Lord announced his victory;
he made his saving power known to the nations.

Psalm 98:1-2 (Sixth Sunday of Easter)

THE WORLD
A marble, an apple, a nice toy, a picture of a new car

Suppose you came home from school and said, "Look what I won in school today!" Then you showed your family this *(the marble)*. What would they say?

Or suppose you said, "Look what I won!" and showed this *(apple)*.

Or suppose you said, "Look what I won!" and showed this *(toy)*.

Or suppose you said, "Look what I won!" and showed this picture *(of a new car)*, then you said, "I won a car. Someone will bring it to our house tonight."

Your family might say, "That's nice," if you won the marble or apple because it's always nice to win something. They would be glad if you won the toy because they'd know you would enjoy it. But a new car! That would be a great prize even for an adult. You would say to everyone, "Look what I won!"

The person who wrote today's psalm says God won something for him. He does not tell us what it is. He only says God won a victory for him. But we can tell by how excited he is that the victory must be something important. Listen to what he says: "Sing a new song to the Lord; he has done wonderful things! By his own power and holy strength he has won the victory. The Lord announced his victory; he has made his saving power known to the nations."

What victory do you think the psalm writer is happy about? Did he run across a snake and kill it? Could be —that would be a victory over something that could have bitten him. Could it be that his family was hungry and he went hunting and killed a deer? That would have been a victory over hunger. Could it be he was in the army? If his side won a battle and he came home alive, that would have been a victory over death.

Or could it be that the man had just come home from worship? He had heard God's message of love and forgiveness. He said, "Look what God gave me. He forgave my sins. He says I am his. I belong to him." What a great victory that would be.

God wins many victories for us. Like the prizes I showed you before, some seem small and some are great. Think of some of the victories God has won for you and how excited you are about each. God gives you food—that is a victory over hunger. He gives you health—a victory over sickness. He gives you family and friends—a victory over loneliness.

All of those are great victories. But God has an even greater victory for you. Jesus came to fight a battle for you. He fought against sin and death. For awhile it looked as if he had lost the battle, because he died. But he rose from the dead! Because Jesus died for your sins, he won the victory for you. Even when you die, you will live again. You can be excited and happy about all the gifts God has won for you. But the greatest is still coming. You will live forever with him!

Clap Your Hands!

THE WORD

Clap your hands for joy, all peoples!
Praise God with loud songs! . . .
God goes up to his throne.
There are shouts of joy and the blast of trumpets,
as the Lord goes up.
Sing praise to God; sing praise to our king!
                    Psalm 47:1, 5-6 (Seventh Sunday of Easter)

THE WORLD

Ask the children (and adults) to participate by clapping

Let me hear you clap. When you clap you show you like someone or something. Now I want you to clap to show us who you know. The rules are this: I will mention a name. If you know of the person, please clap. If you do not know of the person, do not clap. First let's practice. I say, "Santa Claus." You clap because you know of him. I say, "Hannibal Hamlin." He was Abraham Lincoln's first vice president. But I doubt that you know of him, so do not clap.

Are you ready? Clap if you know the person. Don't clap if you don't recognize the name. The first name is *(name a Sunday school teacher that most of the children would know)*. The next name is *(name the parent of a child—one that few others would know)*. The next is *(name the governor of your state or other regional leaders)*. The next is *(name the president or a well-known national leader)*.

Almost *(all)* of you knew *(the Sunday school teacher)*. But do you think the people who live in *(name a nearby town)* would clap for that name?

Probably not. Some of you knew the name of our governor, but most children in *(name a faraway state)* would not know his name. We knew our president's name, but children in Africa would not know him.

Someone can be famous in our congregation and not be known in other places. Even famous people are only known in certain places or in certain times. Let me name one more person. Clap if you recognize the name Jesus Christ.

It's fun to clap for Jesus. There are people all around the world who know Jesus. They have heard the story about Jesus' suffering and death for us. They know he loves all people because he gave himself to be the Savior of all. They know about Jesus because he has invited all people to heaven to be with him forever.

The psalm for today was written for people who knew God. Since they knew him, they clapped for him. Listen to what they said: "Clap your hands for joy, all peoples! Praise God with loud songs! . . . God goes up to his throne. There are shouts of joy and the blast of trumpets, as the Lord goes up. Sing praise to God; sing praise to our king!" When the people came together they blew trumpets and sang songs. They clapped their hands for joy because they knew God. They invited all other people to be happy with them because God loves everyone.

Jesus is the one person that the whole world can clap for. Let's clap for him now.

Don't Live in a Mismatched World

THE WORD

Lord, you have made so many things!
How wisely you made them all!
The earth is filled with your creatures.

Psalm 104:24 (The Day of Pentecost)

THE WORLD

A child's pair of shoes and socks, another large sock and shoe

---

Remember when you woke up this morning? You got out of bed, had breakfast, and got ready for church. Suppose you reached for your socks and grabbed this *(show one child's sock and one large one)*. They don't look as if they belong together, do they? Then when you wanted to put on your shoes you found these *(show one small shoe and one large one)*. Something is wrong here. I have two socks, but they are not a pair of socks. I have two shoes, but they are not a pair of shoes.

This is a pair of socks *(show the child's pair)*. They are the same size and color. They belong together. This is a pair of shoes *(show the child's pair of shoes)*. They belong together for the same reason. If you have socks and shoes that match each other and fit your feet, you can say to the people who made them, "You have made so many things! How wisely you made them!"

But those words were not written for people who make socks and shoes. They were written for God. Psalm 104 says, "Lord, you have made so many things! How wisely you made them all! The earth is filled with your creatures." That was the psalmist's way of saying, "You did a good job, God!"

God showed his wisdom when he made the world. He wanted all the people, the animals, and the plants to live together. Everything was made to match, like socks and shoes that belong together. But we have messed up the world. Instead of living together in peace, people fight with one another. Instead of using the plants and animals in the way God planned, we often misuse and destroy them. When we look at the world today we often think that God's creation doesn't fit together anymore. Things in our world often look like this *(show mismatched socks and shoes)*.

Jesus came to be a part of our world. He saw how people hurt each other, but he came to help. Jesus didn't fit in the world of sin. Everyone thought he was a mismatch, so they killed him.

Jesus was willing to die for us because he wanted to give us a way to live together in peace again. He died to forgive our sins. Then he rose from the dead and sent the Holy Spirit to come to his followers. The Holy Spirit gives us the love and forgiveness that Christ offers to all people. The Holy Spirit brings Jesus into our lives so we can live together in peace again and so we can fit in with all of God's creation.

Often you will see things in the world that do not match. Some people will have lots of food; others will have none. Some will be healthy; others will be sick. Some will know about Jesus as their Savior; others will not. When you see things in the world that do not match, remember God did not make it to be that way. Then remember that God gives you the power of the Holy Spirit—a power that helps you live in God's creation at peace with yourself and others.

You Know Where You Came From

THE WORD
Praise the Lord!
Sing a new song to the Lord;
praise him in the assembly of his faithful people!
Be glad, Israel, because of your Creator.
                    Psalm 149:1-2a (First Sunday after Pentecost)

THE WORLD
A toy in a gift box and a sales slip

Suppose it is your birthday and someone gives you this toy as a gift *(show it)*. It is a good gift and you would enjoy the toy, except for one thing. It is broken. *(Describe something about the toy that could be damaged.)* You can see that it is new but it was broken in its box. You would like to take it back to the store to exchange it for a good toy, but you don't know which store to go to. Even if you found a store that sold toys just like this one, they would not take your broken toy and give you a good one. You would have to prove the toy was bought at their store.

Look at this *(show sales slip)*. I found it in the bottom of the box. This sales slip shows where the toy was purchased. It has the name of the store on it and shows when the toy was bought. You can take the toy back to the store and get a new one—as long as you have the sales slip to prove the toy came from there.

Now I want you to pretend something that may seem funny. But try it anyway. Pretend you are in this box. You are not a toy. You are a person. But you are a gift. Like the toy, you have been hurt. You have

72

sinned. That means you have said and done things you should not have done. Suppose I want to take you back. Where would I take you? I cannot take you back unless I know where you came from.

The people of Israel were happy because they knew where they came from. Listen to the first part of Psalm 149: "Praise the Lord! Sing a new song to the Lord; praise him in the assembly of his faithful people! Be glad, Israel, because of your Creator." God had created them. The people knew they belonged to him. When they needed his help they could go back to him.

You also have been created by God. Besides that, God sent his Son Jesus to be your Savior. Jesus became a person—the only perfect person who lived since people started sinning. Yet Jesus died for us. He took our punishment.

Now when we know we have sinned, we can go back to him. He does not trade us in, like a store that takes back a broken toy and gives a new one. Instead Jesus forgives us. He makes us holy again. Just as he rose from the dead, he also gives us a new life.

You are baptized in the name of Jesus. Think of your Baptism as proof that you belong to him. Then when you have needs you will remember where you came from. You can go back to Jesus and he will claim you. He will help you.

Stay with the One Who Helps You

THE WORD
> When you were in trouble,
> you called to me, and I saved you. . . .
> You must never worship another god.
> I am the Lord your God,
> who brought you out of the land of Egypt.
>   Psalm 81:7a, 9-10a (Second Sunday after Pentecost)

THE WORLD
A bottle of prescription pills and another bottle of pills

Chad had allergies. In the spring when the trees, flowers, and weeds bloomed, he would sneeze and cough all the time. He couldn't go to school or play outside. Chad's parents took him to a doctor. After checking Chad carefully, the doctor ordered these pills for him *(show the prescription pill bottle)*. Every morning Chad took a pill. He stopped sneezing and could go to school again.

One morning Chad grabbed this bottle *(show the nonprescription pills)* instead of the ones the doctor ordered for him. He started sneezing again at school. The next day he took the wrong pills again. His allergies got worse and he had to go home from school. He told his mother he was still taking his pills, but they didn't help any more. After several days his mother discovered he was taking the wrong pills. She gave him the pills the doctor had ordered and Chad became well again.

I told you the story about Chad for two reasons. First, be careful about taking pills. Take only those that the doctor gives you. The other reason is that I hope the story about Chad and the pills will help you remember the lesson from the psalm for today.

In the psalm God says, "When you were in trouble, you called to me, and I saved you." God reminds us that he helps us. The pills that the doctor prescribed helped Chad stop sneezing. God helps us in many ways. He gives us food and health. He sent his son Jesus to save us from sin and death. Because Jesus died for us we are forgiven. When we ask God for help he saves us. He saves us by being with us now. He also saves us because we can live with him forever in heaven.

After God reminds us that he is the one who helps us, he also says, "You must never worship another god. I am the Lord your God, who brought you out of the land of Egypt." Chad had pills that helped him. Then he changed to other pills. He should have kept the ones that helped him. God says he helps you. He tells you not to change to other gods who will not help you. We can make anything into a false god. If you trust something else more than God, you are making it a false god. If you love something else more than God, you are making it a false god.

God wants you to stay with him because he loves you. The false gods cannot love you and take care of you. Stay with Jesus who has promised that he will always stay with you.

Where Can I Hide?

THE WORD

Hear my cry, O God; listen to my prayer!
In despair and far from home I call to you!
Take me to a safe refuge, for you are my protector,
my strong defense against my enemies.

Psalm 61:1-3 (Third Sunday after Pentecost)

THE WORLD

A large cardboard box

Joe was playing in his yard when a big storm came up. The dark clouds, wind, thunder, and lightning scared Joe. He ran into the house and went to his room. He found this box *(show it)* and crawled inside. He felt safe in the box. Would one of you like to crawl into the box? Doesn't it feel nice and safe inside the box? That's how Joe felt. The storm went away.

Later, when Joe was worried or scared, he would crawl inside the box. When his mother was sick, when his father came home late from a trip, Joe crawled into the box. He felt better there.

Then Joe started school. He was away from home. He did not know the teacher or the other boys and girls. He was afraid and wanted to crawl into the box. But the box was far away. He had no place to hide. He was about to cry when he remembered something his mother had read to him from the Bible. It said, "Hear my cry, O God; listen to my prayer! In despair and far from home I call to you! Take me to a safe refuge, for you are my protector, my strong defense against my enemies."

76

Joe remembered what his mother had told him. She said the box did not protect him. She reminded him that God protected him. She told him how Jesus stayed with people who were afraid. Jesus promised to be with people everywhere. Joe knew Jesus loved him. He knew Jesus had died to pay for his sins so he could go to heaven.

Joe thought, "If Jesus wants me in heaven so much he could die for me, he must also want to be with me now." Joe knew he was far from home just like the person who wrote the psalm. He also knew God heard his prayers. He asked God to help him. Instead of crawling into the box, he asked God to be close to him and make him feel better.

Joe wasn't afraid any more. He liked school. After that he didn't need the box anymore. He knew God was with him. He had the box only when he was home, but God was with him everywhere.

I told you the story about Joe so you could remember that God is always with you too. You don't need a place to hide when you are afraid. You don't need a place, instead, you need God. When you want to hide from something that scares you, hide in God. Remember he loves you and is with you. He is your safe refuge—that's a safe place to hide.

Be a Tree

The wicked may grow like weeds,
those who do wrong may prosper;
yet they will be totally destroyed. . . .
The righteous will flourish like palm trees;
they will grow like the cedars of Lebanon.
They are like trees planted in the house of the Lord,
that flourish in the Temple of our God.

Psalm 92:7, 12-13 (Fourth Sunday after Pentecost)

THE WORLD

A large weed and a small seedling tree
(you may use pictures)

These two plants grew side by side. This one *(show the weed)* grew fast and strong. This one *(show the seedling)* is small and slow growing. If you had watched them grow, you would have thought that this one *(weed)* would become a big healthy plant, but that the other would stay little and might even die.

However, that will not happen. This is a weed. No one wants a weed even if it grows big and fast. A weed will either die soon or someone will pull it up to get rid of it. The little plant is a tree. Even though it grows slowly, it will last for a long time. No one will pull it up to get rid of it. Instead people will take care if it. They will water it and trim it so it will become a beautiful tree.

Psalm 92 says people are like plants. First it says, "The wicked may grow like weeds, those who do wrong may prosper; yet they will be totally destroyed." People who do bad things can also enjoy life. They can be healthy. They can have lots of money. They can have friends. But they are like weeds because they don't do any good for anyone but themselves. They don't do anything to help others. When they die, they have done nothing for anyone but themselves.

The same psalm also says, "The righteous will flourish like palm trees; they will grow like the cedars of Lebanon. They are like trees planted in the house of the Lord, that flourish in the Temple of our God." Righteous people are those who do good. They are like trees that produce something for others. Trees give us shade, food, and lumber. We are like trees when we live to give things to others. When we are kind to others, when we help others, we are like trees.

Of course, all of us are like both a weed and a tree. We all have done bad things. We have all done good things. But we can be a tree instead of a weed because Jesus is our Savior. He has forgiven the bad things we did when he died on the cross for us. He gives us his goodness because he gave us his life. Because Jesus was like a tree who grew for us, we have his love and grace so we can be like a tree in the Temple of our God.

You do not have to be afraid or jealous when you see others do bad things and get away with it. Some will cheat and steal and not get caught. But they become like weeds—living only for themselves and hurting others. Because Jesus is with you, you can be like a tree that will not be pulled up or destroyed. Instead you will always live for him.

One God Saves All

THE WORD

"Give thanks to the Lord, because he is good;
his love is eternal!"
Repeat these words in praise to the Lord,
all you whom he has saved.
Psalm 107:1, 2a (Fifth Sunday after Pentecost)

THE WORLD

Several nuts, bolts, and wrenches of various sizes,
including an adjustable wrench

Suppose you were helping your mother fix something around the house. She asks you to get a wrench. You bring this *(show a small wrench)*, but she wants to loosen this *(show a large nut and bolt)*. This wrench won't fit this bolt. So you have to find a large wrench like this *(show large wrench)*. The next time she asks for a wrench you give her the large one, but then she is working on a small bolt like this *(show small bolt)*. Because nuts and bolts come in many sizes like these *(show them)*, we need wrenches in many sizes like these *(show them)*.

However, there is one wrench that will fit all of these bolts. See this? *(Show adjustable wrench.)* I can make the jaws open wide so it will fit the large bolt. Or I can make the jaws small so it will fit the small bolt. One size fits all.

Think of yourself as being a bolt like this *(show a small bolt)*. Think of God as being a wrench. Sometimes we feel that God doesn't fit our needs. He is a wrench like this *(show a large wrench)* that can't come down to our size. Or sometimes we feel we have a big problem *(show large bolt)* and God is a wrench like this *(show a small wrench)*. It seems he can't help us because our problems are too big.

God is like the adjustable wrench. One God can save us all. Listen to the first part of Psalm 197: "Give thanks to the Lord, because he is good; his love is eternal! Repeat these words in praise to the Lord, all you whom he has saved." It says all of us are to praise God because he has saved us. It lists many kinds of people God has saved. Verse 4 says, "Some wandered in the trackless desert." Verse 10 says, "Some were living in gloom and darkness." Verse 17 says, "Some were fools, suffering because of their sins." Verse 23 says, "Some sailed over the ocean in ships." But the same God helped all of these people, so all of them could say, "Give thanks to the Lord, because he is good; his love is eternal!"

All of us share some needs. All of us need food, and God feeds us. "Give thanks to the Lord, because he is good." All of us need the forgiveness of sins. Jesus died to take away our sins. "Give thanks to the Lord, because he is good." All of us will die, and Jesus has promised to bring us back to life again. "Give thanks to the Lord, because he is good."

But each of us have special needs too. Remember, God is like the adjustable wrench. Some people have one problem, some another. Some may have one worry, some another. But one God helps all. "Give thanks to the Lord, because he is good; his love is eternal!"

Look for Something That Lasts

THE WORD

[The Lord's] anger lasts only a moment,
his goodness for a lifetime.
Tears may flow in the night,
but joy comes in the morning.

Psalm 30:5 (Sixth Sunday after Pentecost)

THE WORLD

A balloon and a ball

Look at this balloon and this ball. *(Show them.)* How are they alike? *(Talk about shape, color, and the fact that both are hollow.)* They are alike in many ways. But there is one big difference between the balloon and the ball. How long do you think the balloon will last? How long do you think the ball will last? A balloon lasts only a short time. Some balloons break in a few minutes. The longest any last is only a few days. But you can play with a ball like this for a long time, even for several years.

Look around the room and find some things that last only a short time *(flowers, candles, bulletins, etc.)*. Now find some things that last a long time *(the buildings, altar, furniture, etc.)*.

Now listen to a verse from Psalm 30; "[The Lord's] anger lasts only a moment, his goodness for a life time. Tears may flow in the night, but joy comes in the morning."

God's anger is like the balloon. It lasts only for a short time. God's anger does not mean he hates us. God becomes angry with us for the same reason parents become angry with their children. God loves us and it makes him angry when we do things that hurt ourselves. But God's anger lasts only a moment. It is like the balloon. It pops and goes away. But God's goodness lasts even longer than the balloon or the altar or the building. God's anger lasts only a short time because God has a way to remove our sin that causes his anger. He sent his Son Jesus to be our Savior. Jesus died to pay the punishment for our sin, so our sin is removed. God's anger is gone. *(Break the balloon.)* But God's goodness stays with us forever because Jesus rose from the dead. Jesus is still with us to give us God's goodness. That goodness will always be with us.

Sad things will happen in your life. But your tears will last only for a while. Tears and sorrows are like the balloon; they will go away. But the joys of your life will last forever. Even the tears of death will turn to joy because Jesus will raise us from the dead and take us to heaven. There we will be with him and all others who have received his love.

Look for the things in your life that will last only for a while. Then look for the things that will last forever. Remember it is God's love in Christ that makes forever possible. God takes away the sad things and gives us joy that will last and last.

God Is Always in the Right Mood

THE WORD

Lord, hear my prayer!
In your righteousness listen to my plea;
answer me in your faithfulness!
Don't put me, your servant, on trial;
no one is innocent in your sight.

Psalm 143:1-2 (Seventh Sunday after Pentecost)

THE WORLD

The following words on large pieces of paper: *Busy;
Worried; Relaxed; Righteous; Faithful*

Suppose you want to invite three friends to spend the night at your house. Of course you must ask your parents. But when they come home you can almost see this sign *(busy)* over their heads. One has to go back to work. The other has to go to a meeting. They have to make four phone calls. It is not a good time to ask them to have company. They are busy.

The next night your parents have car trouble on the way home. You can almost see this sign *(worried)* over their heads. Your little brother has a fever. They got lots of bills on the mail. You know it is not a good time to ask for a favor. They are not in the right mood.

The next night your parents come home laughing. You can almost see this sign *(relaxed)* over their heads. They hug you and pat you on your head. They ask what you would like for dinner. Now you know it is the right time to ask if your friends may come over.

You ask your parents for something when they are in the right mood. Do you think God has to be in the right mood to hear your prayer? The person who wrote our psalm for today wanted to ask God for help. He wanted to make sure God was in the right mood. He said, "Don't put me, your servant, on trial; no one is innocent in your sight." He didn't want God to think about all the wrong things he had done. That would not be a good time to ask for help. So the psalmist said, "Lord, hear my prayer! In your righteousness listen to my plea; answer me in your faithfulness."

He wanted God to have this sign *(righteous)* and this one *(faithful)* over his head when he prayed. Righteous means good. When he prayed he wanted God to be in a good mood. Faithful means true or dependable. God is always in the right mood to hear our prayers because he is always good and always faithful. This psalm can help us remember God's good mood so we can always feel free to pray to God. We don't have to wait until God gets in the right mood to hear our prayers. Instead *we* can get in the right mood by remembering how good and faithful God is.

We remind ourselves of God's righteousness and faithfulness when we pray in Jesus' name. God is not only good, he also gives his goodness to us. Jesus died on the cross to pay for our sins. He used his goodness to take away our badness. We are now good in God's eyes because Jesus gave us his goodness. God showed us his faithfulness when he kept his promise and sent Jesus to be our Savior. Jesus is still faithful to us because he is always with us. He helps us. He forgives us. He will be faithful and take us to heaven.

When you want to pray, remember God is always in the mood to hear your prayer. He is always righteous. He is always faithful.

Listen to What God Says

THE WORD

I am listening to what the Lord God is saying;
he promises peace to us, his own people,
if we do not go back to our foolish ways.
Love and faithfulness will meet;
righteousness and peace will embrace.
Man's loyalty will reach up from the earth,
and God's righteousness will look down from heaven.
            Psalm 85:8, 10-11 (Eighth Sunday after Pentecost)

THE WORLD

Coupon from a fast-food restaurant and several dollar bills

Chuck was playing with his video game when his mother left home. She said, "You can buy your lunch today. I put a coupon by the telephone and some money in my drawer." Chuck said, "Yes, Mom." But he was so interested in his game that he didn't listen very well.

When he got hungry Chuck remembered his mother had told him to buy lunch. But he couldn't remember where the coupon and money were. He looked all over and found the coupon *(show it)*. But he couldn't find the money. He couldn't buy lunch because he had not listened to what his mother told him.

The person who wrote the psalm for today knew he could have the same problem if he didn't listen to God. He said, "I am listening to what the Lord God is saying; he promises peace to us, his own people, if we do not go back to our foolish ways." Chuck's mother told him how to buy lunch. God tells us how to have peace. But if we do not listen to what God says, we don't know where to find peace. If we try to find our own peace, we don't receive God's peace.

The psalm also says, "Love and faithfulness will meet; righteousness and peace will embrace." Chuck needed the coupon and the money *(show them)* to buy lunch. The coupon won't buy anything. The money by itself would not buy the lunch Chuck wanted. God also gives us things that go together. We need love and faithfulness. Jesus gave you his love when he died on the cross to pay for your sins. He also gives you faithfulness—that means you can depend on him. He came back to life again and remains with you. When you are with Jesus, love and faithfulness meet. You have both, so you have the peace he gives.

Jesus also gave us his righteousness—that is, his goodness. Because he died for us he gave us his goodness to take away our badness. Since our sin is gone we have peace. His peace and righteousness go together to give us a blessing, just as the coupon and the money together would buy lunch.

The psalm also tells us how we can work together with God. God looks down from heaven with righteousness—remember, that means he sees us in the forgiveness that Jesus gave us. We reach up to him with our loyalty—that is, our faith. Then we have the peace he wants to give us because we believe in him and trust in his goodness.

When we listen to God we know the good news that Jesus is our Savior. Then we have the peace that he wants to give us. Sometimes we are like Chuck. We are too busy to listen to what God says. Then when we need peace we don't know where to find it. I hope you are listening now. God gives you his peace through Jesus Christ.

Jesus Helps You Be You

THE WORD

The Lord is my shepherd; I have everything I need.
He lets me rest in fields of green grass
and leads me to quiet pools of fresh water.
He gives me new strength.
He guides me in the right paths, as he has promised.
                    Psalm 23:1-3 (Ninth Sunday after Pentecost)

THE WORLD

A scissors and a piece of paper

When King David was a young boy he was a shepherd who took care of sheep. The sheep needed a shepherd. Without a shepherd they would get lost or die because they had no food or water.

Since most of you have not seen sheep and shepherds, maybe you can understand it this way. This is a scissors. What is it supposed to do? That's right—scissors are made to cut things. I also have a piece of paper. Can the scissors cut the paper? Sure, but only if someone uses the scissors. Someone has to give it power. Someone has to guide it. See how it cuts when I use it. But it can do nothing by itself.

David knew that sheep were the same way. Someone had to guide and direct the sheep. If a sheep living in a wilderness did not have a shepherd, it would die.

David knew that he was like a sheep. He needed someone to guide him and give him strength. He needed help. By himself he could do nothing right. But he was not by himself. The Lord was his shepherd. The Lord gave him strength. The Lord guided and protected him.

We want to learn the same lesson that King David learned. By ourselves we are like a sheep that will get lost, or like a scissors that can do nothing unless someone uses it. But we do not have to be by ourselves. Jesus has come to be with us. Jesus lived a long time ago, but he can still be with us today because he did something very special for us. He died for us. He gave his life to pay for our sins. When he died he was taken away from us. But he came back to life. He had taken away the one thing that can separate us from each other. He removed death from our lives. Even though he had died, he lived again. He still lives with us.

Jesus is our shepherd. He leads us and protects us. If you think of yourself as the scissors, think of Jesus as the one who gives power to the scissors. Think of him as the one who guides it as it cuts.

We can live by ourselves just as a scissors can be a scissors without cutting anything. But when Jesus is with us, he gives us a purpose for living. We can serve God. We can love and help other people. We can enjoy ourselves. All because Jesus is with us as a shepherd who guides and directs us.

Jesus helps you be you. He helps you enjoy your life here. He promises to take you to heaven with him. He helps you know your life has a purpose.

God's Delivery System

THE WORD
All living things look hopefully to you, [Lord]
and you give them food when they need it.
You give them enough to satisfy the needs of all.
                    Psalm 145:15-16 (Tenth Sunday after Pentecost)

THE WORLD
A can of fruit

I want to give this can of fruit to Amy. *(Name a child far enough away so several children are between you and her.)* I could walk over and give the fruit to Amy. Or I could give it to you. *(Hand the can to the child nearest you.)* You hand it to the next, who hands it to the next, until Amy gets the can. *(Help the children pass the can down the line.)*

Now I am going to ask a question. Think before you answer. Who gave the fruit to Amy? Jeff handed it to her, so he gave it to her. But who gave it to Jeff? Remember how you passed the can from one to the other? Who had the can when we started? Even though many of you handed the can down the line, I gave it to Amy. Right?

Maybe not. Where did I get the can of fruit? Just as you handed it from one to the other, someone had to hand it to me. I got it from the grocery store. But the fruit didn't start in the store. It started in an orchard. It passed from those who picked it to those who canned it to those who brought it to the store. So if you follow the fruit back to its beginning you find who gave it to Amy. Not Jeff. Not me. Not the grocery store. Not the person who owned the orchard. Finally it has to go back to God. The fruit grew on a tree. God created the tree. God gave the water, the sun, and the soil to make it grow. So God gave the fruit. He gave it through many people, but each of them passed it on from one to the other.

King David knew the food he ate did not come from the people who brought it to his table. He knew he did not earn his food because he was rich and strong. King David said, "All living things look hopefully to you, [Lord] and you give them food when they need it. You give them enough to satisfy the needs of all." When David ate his food he could look beyond the servants, the cooks, and the farmers who prepared his food. He saw their work as a gift of God, and he knew God fed him.

God also gives us many other gifts through people. I can tell you about the greatest gift of all. God loves you. Jesus has died for you to forgive your sins. He rose from the dead to give you eternal life. God's love is the greatest gift. I can tell you about it, but it does not come from me. Someone else told me, and I know God loves me. Now I can pass it on to you. When you receive the love Jesus has given you, you can also pass it on to others.

God Gives Us More than We Ask For

THE WORD

So the people ate and were satisfied;
God gave them what they wanted.

Psalm 78:29 (Eleventh Sunday after Pentecost)

THE WORLD

Two souvenir items

Chad was on vacation with his family. His parents said he could buy one souvenir to take home. At the first stop he saw this flag *(show souvenir flag or substitute some other item)* and wanted it for his room. He asked his parents to buy it. They suggested he wait a while because he might see something that he would rather have. But Chad was sure. He wanted the flag. So his parents bought it for him.

At the next stop Chad saw this billfold *(show billfold or substitute some other item)*. If he had it he could take it to school with him. Then all of his friends could see it. The flag was nice, but only those who came to his home would see it. When he asked his parents to buy the billfold, they reminded him that he could buy only one souvenir.

Chad was disappointed. He liked the flag, but he wished he had waited and bought the billfold instead.

I told you the story about Chad to help you understand the psalm for today. It tells about the people of Israel when they were traveling in a desert. They did not have much food. They complained to Moses and to God because they were hungry. All they wanted was food. God gave them a special bread and he sent birds so they had meat to eat. The psalm says, "So the people ate and were satisfied; God gave them what they wanted."

Every day they had bread and meat. For a few days they were happy. Then they wanted something else to eat. They complained again. They were like Chad. When they got what they wanted, they wanted something else.

All of us are like Chad and the people of Israel. When we want something, it seems very important to us. But when we get it, we start thinking about other things we'd like to have. If we get the other things, we will want still more. When we let ourselves think that way, we never enjoy what we do have because we are always looking at what we do not have.

But we can change. Let's go back to the story about Chad. While on vacation Chad kept thinking about what he was going to buy. He forgot to enjoy his vacation with his parents. He was not happy because they loved him and wanted to buy a gift for him. Instead of enjoying his parents, he thought only of what they might buy him.

The Israelites did the same thing. They thought about the food they needed. But they forgot God, who gave them the food. Instead of thanking God for the special bread and the meat, they wanted to look at the menu and order something else.

God gives you many great gifts. Thank him for the gifts and enjoy them. Feel free to ask him for blessings. Remember, God gives them to you because he loves you. God doesn't give you just food and other things you need and want. He also gives you himself. He sent his Son Jesus to be your Savior. Jesus gave himself for you when he died on the cross to pay for your sins. Jesus is still with you because he rose from the dead. God has given us even more than we ask for. He has given us himself.

Use Your Spiritual Senses

THE WORD
Find out for yourself how good the Lord is.
Psalm 34:8a (Twelfth Sunday after Pentecost)

THE WORLD
A bottle of perfume that a child might give to a mother

Suppose you want to buy a present for your mother. Maybe it's her birthday, or maybe you just want to give her a gift. What should you give her? You go to a store and shop. Look. Here is some perfume. *(Show the bottle.)* It is a pretty bottle, but you wonder. Will your mother like it? The lady tells you that it smells good—like roses in the morning. That sounds good. But perfume does not have to sound good. It has to smell good.

Then the clerk asks if you would like to smell the perfume. She takes the cap off and lets you smell it. *(Let each child smell the perfume.)* When the clerk told you it smelled good, you knew what she thought about the perfume. But now that you have smelled it, you know what you think about it. If you like it, you can buy it for your mother.

I've talked to you about how you learn about perfume. The psalm for today tells us how to learn about God. It says, "Find out for yourself how good the Lord is."

Many people will tell you about God. That is good. I like to tell you that Jesus loves you. I like to tell you that Jesus is your Savior because he died to pay for your sins. I hope you like to hear that Jesus rose from the dead and is still alive today.

But the psalm writer tells you to find out for yourself. How do you find out about God? If you want to find out about perfume, you smell it. If you want to find out about food, you taste it. You touch some things to find out about them. You look at others. But how do you find out about God?

Our bodies help us understand the things we can see, hear, touch, smell, and taste. We use our eyes, ears, fingers, noses, and mouths. Those are all parts of our bodies. But God is a Spirit. To understand God we cannot depend on the senses of our bodies. We need to use the senses of our spirits.

Some of your spiritual senses are love, hope, faith, and joy. You and I can feel those things just as we also feel and know things with the senses of our body. God tells us that he has made both things that we can see and the things that we cannot see. Our regular senses can help us know about the things we can see. But it takes our spiritual senses to know about the things we cannot see. We learn about God through our spiritual senses.

Because God loves us, we can feel love for him. Because God gives us his grace in Christ, we can have faith in him. Because God promises to be with us always, we can have hope and joy. Others may tell you about God. But you learn about God for yourself when you feel in your spirit the things God feels for you. When you know he gives himself to you, you also know who he is because you have felt his presence.

Have Reverence for the Lord

THE WORD

Come, my young friends, and listen to me,
and I will teach you to have reverence for the Lord.
Psalm 34:11 (Thirteenth Sunday after Pentecost)

THE WORLD

A national flag in a paper sack

Today's psalm says, "Come, my young friends, and listen to me." You are my young friends. I have invited you to come and be with me. I also ask you to listen to me. The psalm tells you why I want you to listen to me. It says, "and I will teach you to have reverence for the Lord." I have invited you, my young friends, to listen to me, because I want to teach you to have reverence for the Lord.

Reverence means to have respect for, to feel good about something, to take good care of something. See this sack? *(Show it.)* There's nothing special about a plain brown bag like this. I do not have reverence for the sack, and I don't expect you to have reverence for it either. If you were carrying this sack, you might drop it in a trash can. Or you might throw it to one of your friends. You might even let it fall in a puddle of water.

Now let me show you what is in the sack. What is this? *(Show the flag.)* The flag is important to us. It reminds us of our country. The flag helps us think of the many blessings God has given us in our country. *(Put the flag back in the sack.)* Now would you drop the sack in a trash can? Would you throw it in a puddle of water? Of course not. When you know what is

96

in the sack, you show your respect to the flag by taking good care of the sack.

Remember, I invited you here to teach you to have reverence for the Lord. Just as I have the flag in a sack, God also comes to us in ways that we can accept him as a part of our world even though we don't see him. God became a person in Jesus Christ and he lived on earth with other people. Many people who saw him thought he was just another person. They argued with him. They made fun of him. They finally killed him. They didn't have reverence for Jesus because they did not see God in the man, just as some might not know the flag is in the sack.

But you know about Jesus. You know he died for you and he is still alive today. You show your reverence for God by the way you speak about him and to him. When you speak God's name you show him and others that you respect him.

Jesus comes to us today through his word that we read in the Bible. Jesus is with us when we join with others in worshiping God and in serving him in the church. We show our reverence for God by the way we use his word and by the way we treat others who also believe in him. Just as the sack contains the flag, the Bible brings us the good news about Jesus, and the church gives us a way to be with Jesus.

Remember Your Return Address

THE WORD

The good man suffers many troubles,
but the Lord saves him from them all. . . .
The Lord will save his people;
those who go to him for protection will be spared.
     Psalm 34:19, 22 (Fourteenth Sunday after Pentecost)

THE WORLD

Two letters with address labels, one with a return address

These two letters *(show them)* are addressed to someone in another city. They were dropped in a mailbox. But something bad happened to them. They got caught in the mailbox and the addresses were torn off. *(Remove the address labels and throw them away.)* When the postal clerks found the letters, they did not know where to send them.

Both letters had the same problem, but there is a difference. See, this letters has a return address. But this one does not. The post office returned this letter to the person who sent it. The sender then put a new address on the letter and mailed it again. This time it was delivered to the person to whom it was addressed. But the other letter has no return address. The people at the post office had no place to send it. They had to throw it away.

I didn't tell you about these letters to teach you to put a return address on your letters when you mail them. Instead, I want you to learn something about yourself. Each of us is like these letters. The letters had problems—they lost their addresses. We have problems. We do wrong things that hurt others. Others do wrong things that hurt us. We get sick. We are afraid. We worry. Those problems are to us like losing an address is to a letter.

But what happens to us when we have problems? Do we get thrown away, like this letter? Or can we have help, like this letter? Before we answer those questions, let's listen to what the psalm for today says: "The good man suffers many troubles, but the Lord saves him from them all. . . . The Lord will save his people; those who go to him for protection will be spared."

We have troubles, but we have a place to go for help. We have a return address. When Jesus died to pay for our sins and when he rose from the dead to give us eternal life, he became a part of our lives. He put his name on us, just as a return address is on this letter.

Even though Jesus is our Savior, we still have problems. We still sin. We are still hurt by the sins of others. But those problems will not destroy us. We will not be thrown away. Each time we have a problem, we go back to the return address—we go back to God. Because Jesus is our Savior, God forgives us. Because he loves us, he helps us start over again.

When you have problems, remember this promise, "The Lord will save his people; those who go to him for protection will be spared." You have a place to go for help. Go back to God who created you and who saved you.

Who Can Come to Church?

THE WORD

Lord, who may enter your Temple?
Who may worship on Zion, your sacred hill?
A person who obeys God in everything
and always does what is right,
whose words are true and sincere,
and who does not slander others.
                    Psalm 15:1-3a (Fifteenth Sunday after Pentecost)

THE WORLD

Three plates, each smeared with mustard, and a damp
cloth

Psalm 15 asks two questions: "Lord, who may enter your Temple? Who may worship on Zion, your sacred hill?" Today we would ask the questions this way: Lord, who can come to church? Who can worship you?

How would you answer those questions? We invite everyone to church. We want all people to worship God. But listen to the answer in the psalm; "A person who obeys God in everything and always does what is right, whose words are true and sincere, and who does not slander others."

That answer scares us. What if the ushers stood at our church door and checked everyone who came. What if they asked you: Have you obeyed God in everything? Do you always do what is right? Do you always tell the truth? Have you said anything bad about others?

If we had to pass a test like that, none of us would be able to come to church. But remember, God wants us to worship him. He helps us pass the test. Let me show you something so you can see how God helps us pass the test. Suppose your mother told you to put away these dishes. *(Show the plates.)* But she says to put away only the clean dishes. Look at this plate. Can you put it away? See the mess on it. And this one. Look at this one. None of them are clean. So you can't put any away. In the same way all of us have done wrong things, so none of us can worship.

However, there is a way you can put these dishes away. First you clean the dishes. *(Wipe the plates clean with the cloth.)* See, this plate is clean now. You can put it away. Now this one is clean. So is this one. You can put them all away.

We can all come to worship God. We can invite all other people to come with us. The ushers will not ask anyone if they have sinned. Instead God asks us. And God also cleans us. God sent his Son Jesus to be our Savior. Jesus died for our sins so we can be forgiven. He has made us clean because he take the sins off of us and puts them on himself, just as the mess went off the plates and on the cloth.

When we come to church to worship, we start by asking God to forgive our sins. We know we need to be made clean so we can worship. Then we hear the message about Jesus. We know he forgives us. We are made clean. Then we can all worship him. We worship him because we have received his love and we want to give him our love.

Who Will Protect You?

THE WORD

Praise the Lord! Praise the Lord, my soul!
I will praise him as long as I live;
I will sing to my God all my life.
Don't put your trust in human leaders;
no human being can save you.

Psalm 146:1-3 (Sixteenth Sunday after Pentecost)

THE WORLD

Six cookies, a paper bag, and a metal canister

Suppose your mother gave you these cookies *(show them)* to take on a school field trip. You can't carry the cookies in your hands, can you? You need something to hold them. What about this bag? *(Put the cookies in the sack.)* Now you can carry them easily and you won't lose them.

But what will happen if you drop the sack of cookies? They might fall out. Or even worse—what if someone sits on the sack while you are on the bus? You'd have cookie crumbs instead of cookies. The sack helps you carry the cookies, but it does not protect them.

This will help. *(Put the sack in the canister.)* Now the cookies are well protected. You still have the sack to help you carry the cookies when you take them from the can. The can will protect them from bumps and falls.

Can you think of yourself as being like these cookies? You can also be hurt. You can be hurt by cuts, bruises, and broken bones. Even more than that, you can be hurt by words and actions. You can be sad and lonely.

You can worry and be afraid. Just as the cookie needs protection, so do you.

The sack can remind you of the people who want to help you. The sack is your parents, your teachers, your friends. I also want to help you. The people who take care of you, who teach you, and who help you all love you. But all of us will let you down at one time or another. We will not always be there when you need us. We will not always know how to help you. Or we will be busy with something else. That's why the psalm warns us by saying, "Don't put your trust in human leaders; no human being can save you." Other people love you and want to help you, but they cannot always give you the help you need. They are like the paper sack.

But listen to what else the psalm says: "Praise the Lord! Praise the Lord, my soul! I will praise him as long as I live; I will sing to my God all my life." God is the one who can help you. He is like this can. People may help you know God. Just as the sack holds the cookies as they go into the can, people who love you can help you know that God loves you even more.

I hope you can always love other people and let them love you. You can also trust them—but you can trust them only as much as they are able to help you. All people are limited in helping you because they also need help. All humans are limited except one— that one is Jesus. Jesus is God who also became a human being. He became like us to die for us and to give us new life. But he also is God. So he has no limits on his ability to help you.

Think of the people who help you as being the sack and Jesus as the can. The people help you know Jesus, but he is the only one who protects you.

Someone Who Listens

THE WORD

I love the Lord, because he hears me;
he listens to my prayers.
He listens to me every time I call to him.
  Psalm 116:1-2 (Seventeenth Sunday after Pentecost)

THE WORLD

A cassette tape recorder and a tape

When I speak, the words come out of my mouth. Then they go through the air to your ears. When you speak, the words come from your mouth and go to my ears. If you were alone and you said something, the words would come out of your mouth, but there would be no ears to hear the words.

This machine *(show a tape recorder without a tape)* also has ears. See this microphone? It receives words just as ears do. I must push these buttons to make the machine hear words. *(Do it.)* The psalm for today says, "I love the Lord, because he hears me; he listens to my prayers. He listens to me every time I call to him."

Now I push rewind, then I push the play button. *(Do it.)* But we don't hear anything. I spoke words. The words went into the microphone. But there was no tape in the machine. It could receive the words but it could not record them. Now I'll put the tape in. Again I'll push the right buttons and read the psalm. *(Do it.)* Let's see if the machine heard my words this time. *(Rewind the tape and play it.)*

Sometimes we listen to each other as though we were tape recorders without tapes. The words go in our ears, but we don't pay any attention to them. I'm sure you sometimes think your mothers, fathers, or schoolteachers don't pay any attention to you when you are talking. Your words go in their ears but don't get recorded. I should tell you that your mothers, fathers, and teachers also think there are times when they speak to you and you do not listen to them.

Remember the words I read from the psalm? They tell us God not only hears, but he also listens to us. The psalmist said he loved God because God always heard his prayers. God always listened to him. The person who wrote the psalm knew other people didn't always pay attention to him. But God did. God listened to every word he said.

God also listens to you. The words do not just go in God's ear and disappear. The words go to God's heart. Think of this tape in the recorder as being Jesus. When we pray to God the words become a part of Jesus. He listens and he cares.

Because Jesus loves us, he was willing to die for us. Yet he can still hear us because he came back to life again. If he loved you so much that he would die to pay for your sins, he also loves you enough to listen to everything you say. He is never too busy to hear you. He does not forget you. Jesus will not give you everything you ask for, because sometimes he knows a better way to help you. But he always hears and he always cares.

You Can't Pay God

THE WORD

I will gladly offer you a sacrifice, O Lord;
I will give you thanks because you are good.
You have rescued me from all my troubles.
          Psalm 54:6-7a (Eighteenth Sunday after Pentecost)

THE WORLD

A dollar bill and a card made by a child that says,
"Thank you. I love you."

Suppose you stopped at a store to buy something to drink. After the clerk served you the drink, he would hold out his hand. You would know he expected to be paid for the drink. You have these two things with you. *(Show them.)* One is a dollar bill. The other is a card you made. You colored it yourself and you wrote the message, "Thank you. I love you." Which one do you think the clerk would want? He served you the drink. He is expecting you to pay for it. He would not want the card. He would want the dollar bill.

Now I'll tell you another pretend story. Suppose your father and mother take you to the park. You have a picnic. You play a game. Maybe you see the animals in the zoo. Your parents push you in the swing. It is a fun day. When you come home, you go to your room and get these same two things. Which one do you think you should give to your mother and father? Would they rather have the dollar or the card you made? You know they'd rather have the card. They do not want to be paid for what they did for you. But it would make them happy if you thanked them by giving them the card you made.

Now I'll tell a story that is not pretend, but real. God loves you. He sent his Son Jesus to be your Savior. Jesus forgives all your sins because he died for you. He rose from the dead and promises you that you can live with him forever. Again you have these two things in your hand—the dollar and the card. Which one would God rather have from you?

Before you answer the question, let me read you something from Psalm 54. It says, "I will gladly offer you a sacrifice, O Lord; I will give you thanks because you are good. You have rescued me from all my troubles."

You cannot pay God for what he has done for you. You could pay the clerk for the drink. You can pay for food and games and tickets. You can buy things from friends. But you can't pay God.

However, you can thank God. You can say thank you to him in your prayers and in the songs you sing. You can also give him a sacrifice. You could use the dollar as a sacrifice. You would not give it to God to pay him, but you could give it to someone who would use it to buy food for a hungry person. You could give it to a missionary who would tell other people that Jesus loves them. You can give it as a sacrifice to say thanks to God. God is like your mother and father. He does not want to be paid. But he likes to be thanked.

The Same God Forever

Lord, you will always be proclaimed as God;
all generations will remember you.
> Psalm 135:13 (Nineteenth Sunday after Pentecost)

THE WORLD
In the United States: a picture of the current president
and pictures of several previous presidents (from mag-
azine covers or children's history books). In other countries change to respective national leaders.

Do you know who this is? *(Show picture of current
president.)* This is a picture of the president of the
United States. His name is _____. Do you know
who this is? *(Show a former president.)* This is
_____. He was the president of the United
States in *(name years and relate to the lives of the
children and their parents. Show other pictures of
presidents. Give the name and time in history when
each served.)*

Our country always has only one president. But 38
(1984 figure) different people have been president of
the United States.

In all of creation we also have only one God. Only
we do not get a new God every few years or few
centuries. The God we worship today is the same
God who always has been and always will be. Listen
to what Psalm 135 says: "Lord, you will always be
proclaimed as God; all generations will remember
you."

The person who wrote this psalm worshiped the
same God his family had worshiped for thousands of

years. He knew that the people who lived after him would keep on worshiping the same God. We live almost 3000 years later. We still worship the same God as the psalm writer did long ago.

Think of other things that have changed. Our country did not exist then. The countries that did exist then are gone now. The way we work, eat, and go to school are very different from a long time ago. But God is still God. He is always the same God.

God shows us today that he is the same God as he was long ago because he wants to stay with the people he created. From the beginning people have tried to run away from God. But God knows we need him. We need him so much he even sent his Son Jesus to live with us. But the people at that time didn't want God to be with them. They were just like the people who had lived before Jesus came and the people who have lived since then. So they killed God's Son. When they killed him, he became a sacrifice to pay for the sin that made them do such a terrible thing. He died for the sins of all people.

But even Jesus's death did not separate God from his people. Jesus came back to life. He still lives with us.

God has always been God, and God will always be God. We live in a time that is changing very quickly. The way you live when you grow up will be different from the way your parents live now. Your school is different from the school that your parents went to. Sometimes people have a difficult time living with all the changes. Remember Psalm 135, verse 13. God will always be God. Even though the world has changed in many ways during the past, we have not had to change gods. The world will continue to change. But we have a God who will continue to be God.

Happy Are Those Who Obey

THE WORD

Happy are those who have reverence for the Lord,
who live by his commands.
Psalm 128:1 (Twentieth Sunday after Pentecost)

THE WORLD

Two face masks cut from paper; crayons, string, and
tape

Gail and Chris were making masks for Halloween
in an art class at school. They wanted to wear the
masks when they went out for trick or treat. The
teacher told them to cut out the masks like this. *(Show
the masks.)* Then the teacher said to color the masks.
(Make some bold marks on the masks.) The girls did
that. Then the teacher told them to add the string to
the masks so they could tie them on their heads and
to put tape around the place where the string was tied
to the mask.

Gail put on the string and carefully put tape around
it. *(Do it.)* But Chris was in a hurry. She knew no
one would see the tape anyway because it doesn't show.
So she put on the string and rushed out to recess without using the tape.

When the two girls went out on Halloween, each
wore her mask. But Chris's mask soon fell off. The
string had pulled the paper and torn it. *(Pull on the
string and tear it lose.)* Gail's mask stayed on because
she had followed the teacher's instructions. The tape
made a strong place on the paper so it did not tear
loose. Chris did not have any tape with her to fix the

mask. She did not enjoy Halloween because she had no mask. Gail had a good time.

Sometimes we ignore God's laws just like Chris ignored what the teacher told her to do with the tape. God tells us how to live because he knows what is best for us and because he loves us. But often we are too busy to do what God asks us to do. Or we would rather do what we think is best for ourselves instead of what God says is best for us. But when we do not follow God's laws, we cause problems for ourselves and for others. Things don't turn out right when we don't live the way God tells us to live.

The psalm for today says, "Happy are those who have reverence for the Lord, who live by his commands." Gail had more fun on Halloween than Chris because she followed the teacher's rules and Chris did not. Those who follow God's rules will also enjoy life more than those who do not.

But we have a problem. We cannot follow all of God's laws. We cannot do everything he told us to do. We cannot avoid doing some of the things he told us not to do. However, God still loves us. He wants us to be happy. So he sent Jesus to be our Savior. Jesus died and took the punishment for our sin. Now he lives again to give us his goodness.

Because Jesus is our Savior we can be happy. He has obeyed the laws of God for us. With his help we can also now obey the laws more than we could before. Jesus loves us and helps us do the things that are good and avoid the things that are bad.

When you hear God's laws, remember God wants to help you. He wants to make you happy and to make other people happy. The psalm says, "Happy are those who have reverence for the Lord, who live by his commands."

How to Start the Day

THE WORD
Fill us each morning with your constant love,
so that we may sing and be glad all our life.
Psalm 90:14 (Twenty-First Sunday after Pentecost)

THE WORLD
A girl's purse, comb, facial tissue, money, house key

Gail saw other girls her age carrying purses, so she wanted one too. She asked her mother and father to buy a purse for her. Her parents agreed and gave Gail this purse *(show it)* for her birthday. She was happy to have it and took it with her to church, school, and other places.

Gail liked the purse because it looked nice. She never put anything in it because she wanted to keep it exactly the way it was when it was new. One day at school she had the sniffles, but she did not have any tissue with her. That was embarrassing. Another day she lost her offering for Sunday school because she carried the coins in her hand. Another time she forget her house key and had to sit on the doorstep to wait for her mother to come home from work.

Gail had wanted the purse only because it would look nice. Then she discovered that she needed a purse to carry things. Every morning Gail would put what she needed for the day in her purse. She would put in this comb, some tissues, her spending money, her house key, and anything else that she might need that day *(show these items)*. The purse was a big help to her.

In one way you are like Gail's purse. You can have things put in you. I don't mean food that you eat. I mean you can have feelings and ideas put inside you just as Gail put things in her purse. Listen to Psalm 90: "Fill us each morning with your constant love, so that we may sing and be glad all our life."

The person who wrote the psalm was praying to God. He asked God to fill him with love each morning. Remember the things Gail put in her purse? Those were the things she needed that day. Think of yourself as you wake up in the morning. What kind of feelings and ideas are going to be in you during the day? Will you be grouchy or cheerful? Will you be excited or bored? Will you be worried or happy? All of us have good days and bad days. Many times our days are bad days because we start the day in a bad way.

The way to make a day a good day is to start by filling yourself with the things you need to make a good day. Remember the psalm that asks God to fill us with love so we can be glad all day long.

God gives you the love you need. Start the day by remembering that Jesus loves you. Jesus used to live on this earth just like you do. He woke up in the morning and said "Good morning" to his family and friends. You can say "Good morning" to your family and friends in the way Jesus did. When Jesus puts his love in you, you can give love to others.

As you begin each day, remember that Jesus is alive and with you. Even though he died to pay for our sins, he came back to life and is with you now. Remember that you are baptized in his name. He has made you clean from sin and has given you a new life. You are filled with his love and you can use it all day long. Tomorrow he will fill you with love again.

Help That You Can't See

THE WORD
> God will put his angels in charge of you
> to protect you wherever you go.
> They will hold you up with their hands
> to keep you from hurting your feet on the stones.
> Psalm 91:11-12
> (Twenty-Second Sunday after Pentecost)

THE WORLD
> A cardboard box (large enough to hold a child) with *Protection* written on one side

---

Do you know this word? *(Show the box.)* The word is *protection*. To *protect* means to "keep safe." Your mother and father love you so they want to protect you from danger. God loves you so he also wants to protect you. Let's look at two ways you could be protected.

I'll show you one of the ways to protect you. Mike, come here. I'll put you in this box. *(Do it.)* As long as you are in the box you are protected from car wrecks and playground accidents. If you are in the box you are protected from people who would hurt you. While you are in the box you are protected from hearing and seeing bad things that could hurt you.

Do you like to be protected this way, Mike? If I kept you in the box I would protect you from danger. But I would also keep you from enjoying life. You couldn't run and play. You couldn't go to school or be a part of your family. That kind of protection would hurt you.

But God has another way to protect you. Instead of putting *you* in the protection, he puts the *protection* in you. Step out of the box, Mike. Listen to Psalm 91:11-12: "God will put his angels in charge of you to protect you wherever you go. They will hold you up with their hands to keep you from hurting your feet on the stones."

Instead of protecting you by putting you in a box, God puts faith inside you. He tells you he sends his angels to guard and protect you. I can't show you an angel like I can show you this box. But angels are just as real as the box is. God sends his angels to be with us wherever we go. God does not protect us by locking us up so we can't get into trouble. Instead he goes with us to help us at all times.

When Jesus came to live on earth, God sent angels to help him just as he sends angels to help us. The people who lived then could see and talk to Jesus. But they could not see the angels. Yet Jesus knew the angels were there. They gave him hope and comfort.

Even though the angels were with him, Jesus died. Because Jesus died, we see the greatness of God's protection for us. Jesus came back to life again. Because Jesus did all this for us, we know that when we die we will live again.

We can't see the angels with us. But they are there to protect us. God gives us faith in him so we can know about his protection. He will always be with us to take care of us.

A Dream Come True

THE WORD
> When the Lord brought us back to Jerusalem,
> it was like a dream!
> How we laughed, how we sang for joy!
> Then the other nations said about us,
> "The Lord did great things for them."
>> Psalm 126:1-2 (Twenty-Third Sunday after Pentecost)

THE WORLD
> Three large cards with the following: *J sus, Je us, Jes s.*

Can you read this? *(Show first card.)* You may be able to read it, but something is missing. What has been left out? This card needs an E to make it complete.

What is missing from this card? *(Show the second.)* It needs an S to make it spell the word *Jesus*. What about this card? *(Show the third.)* Again, you can read it, but it needs a U.

Each of the cards I showed you had four letters on it. Each was also missing one letter. We paid more attention to the letter that was missing than the four letters that were there. In our lives we often pay more attention to what we do not have than what we do have.

Will all of you close your eyes for a minute? Pretend you are blind. If you were blind, the most important thing to you would be to be able to see again. Now open your eyes. You can see. Isn't it wonderful to be able to see other people? For a person who is really blind, the gift of sight would be a dream come true. Seeing is a beautiful gift. But as long as we can see we seldom think about it. Instead we think about what we do not have.

The child who lives with only a mother or a father thinks that having both parents would solve all problems. The person who is crippled thinks that being healthy would solve all problems. The poor person thinks having money would solve all problems. Each has a dream that he wants to come true. But each person may forget that the person who has both parents, the one who is healthy, the one who has money—all still have other problems.

The people in our psalm had a dream that came true. They had been slaves in a foreign country. Then they were freed and went back to their own land again. They said, "When the Lord brought us back to Jerusalem, it was like a dream! How we laughed, how we sang for joy! Then the other nations said about us, 'The Lord did great things for them.' "

For a while the people were happy because their dream had come true. They were free again. Then they began to see other problems. They worried about other things. They forgot how happy they were to be free in their own land.

Do you ever forget how wonderful it is that Jesus is your Savior? Before I asked you to pretend you were blind. Then it was a joy to see again. Now pretend you do not have a Savior. Pretend Jesus has not died for you, so you must pay for your own sin. Pretend Jesus did not come alive again and go to heaven, so there is no one to take you to heaven. Pretend he is not with you to help you. Then you would dream how nice it would be to have a Savior.

But the dream has come true. Jesus did die to pay for your sins. He is alive. He is with you and loves you. He will take you to heaven. The dream comes true every day because Jesus has promised he will never leave you.

God Will Help You Obey

THE WORD

How can a young man keep his life pure?
By obeying your commands.
With all my heart I try to serve you;
keep me from disobeying your commandments.

Psalm 119:9-10
(Twenty-Fourth Sunday after Pentecost)

THE WORLD

A list of "commandments" (see below), a candle, and matches

Jennifer, would you help me teach the psalm for today? The psalm asks a question: "How can a young man keep his life pure?" It also gives an answer, "By obeying your commands." It says if we want to be good we will obey God's commands.

But that is hard to do. Jennifer, I have a list of commandments. *(Show it.)* These are not God's commands; I made them up. But I want you to obey the commands I wrote. Here they are:

1. Shake hands with Billy.

2. Smile at Kathryn.

3. Wave at your mother.

4. Light that candle (one too high for the child to reach).

Now, Jennifer, will you do those things? You may have forgotten some of the things I asked you to do. You don't have a match and you can't reach the candle. What should you do when you cannot obey the commands I gave?

Let me tell you what the psalm writer did. He said, "With all my heart I try to serve you; keep me from disobeying your commandments." First, he said he tried with all his heart. You tried too, didn't you, Jennifer? Then the psalm writer asked God to help him obey the commandments.

If you can't obey the commands I gave, you can ask me for help. Did you forget some of them? I'll tell you again. *(Repeat the first three and help her do them one at a time.)* God will also help you remember the commands he gives. We teach the Bible in our worship service to remind you of what God has told you to do. We ask you to go to Sunday school and to read the Bible at home so you will remember what God told you. If you don't know what God asks you to do, ask him to help you. He will help you obey.

The last command I gave you was to light the candle. Even if you remember that command, you can't do it. But you can ask me for help. I have a match. I will move the candle so you can reach it. Now you can light the candle because I was with you and helped you.

We cannot obey all of God's commands either— even if we remember them. But we can ask God to help us. He sent Jesus to obey the commandments for us. Jesus died to forgive us when we disobeyed God. He came back from the grave to live with us and to help us. Jesus will help you forgive people even when you can't forgive by yourself. He will help you love even when you can't love by yourself. God will help you obey his commands.

You Can Say That Again

THE WORD

"Give thanks to the Lord, because he is good;
his love is eternal!"
Repeat these words in praise to the Lord,
all of you whom he has saved.
    Psalm 107:1-2a (Twenty-Fifth Sunday after Pentecost)

THE WORLD

A local telephone book, a Bible

How many of you know a telephone number? Do you know your own phone number? What other numbers do you know? *(See if they know police or emergency numbers. Discuss the numbers they know and why they have memorized them.)*

Do you know the phone number of the church? Do you know the number to call? *(Name local businesses or recreation places that the children would recognize.)* You know some numbers, but there are many more that you do not know. But you can still call those other places. All of the numbers are in this telephone book *(show it)*. You can look up the numbers that you do not use often. But you don't need to look up the numbers you use often; you know them.

Here is another book *(show the Bible)* that has things in it you need to know. If you want to read the story about the birth of Jesus, you can find it in here. If you want to know how he died as a sacrifice to pay for the sins of the world, you can look it up in here. If you want to read how Jesus rose from the dead and promised to be with you always, you can read it in here.

You can look up many other things in the Bible.

But some things in the Bible are like your own phone number. You use them so often that you don't have to look them up anymore. You know them by heart. Listen to these words from Psalm 107: "Give thanks to the Lord, because he is good; his love is eternal!" Every morning when you wake up you could say, "Give thanks to the Lord, because he is good; his love is eternal!" After every meal you could thank God for the food by saying, "Give thanks to the Lord, because he is good; his love is eternal!" Many other times when you are happy or when you remember how good God is you can say, "Give thanks to the Lord, because he is good; his love is eternal!" Just as it is worth learning your phone number because you use it often, it is worthwhile for you to learn this prayer of thanksgiving because you have many reasons to thank God.

The person who wrote this psalm liked to say, "Give thanks to the Lord, because he is good; his love is eternal!" His next words are, "Repeat these words in praise to the Lord, all of you whom he has saved."

The psalm writer thinks that everyone who has been saved should say over and over again, "Give thanks to the Lord, because he is good; his love is eternal!" You are saved because Jesus saved you. He has promised to take you to heaven. He has promised to be with you on earth. Why don't you thank him with me? Let's say it together, "Give thanks to the Lord, because he is good; his love is eternal!" You can say that again!

I Like to Be with You

THE WORD

> You will show me the path that leads to life;
> your presence fills me with joy
> and brings me pleasure forever.
> Psalm 16:11 (Twenty-Sixth Sunday after Pentecost)

THE WORLD

Five socks of different sizes and colors and one pair of matched socks

---

Your father has done the laundry. Your job is to put the clothes away. First you have to match up the socks. You start with this one *(show one sock from the matched pair)*. Would these two make a pair? *(Put the sock with a larger one of a different color.)* No, they don't belong together. What if you had one foot this size, the other this size? Would you want to wear one sock this color and one this color?

So let's look for another sock. *(Continue to match other socks with the first. Comment on why they are not mates.)* What about this one? *(This time show the matching sock.)* These two are the same size. They are the same color. They are made of the same material. They are a pair.

Now let's pretend you are this sock *(show one from the pair)*. We are looking for a mate for you. How do you find someone who matches you? The person who wrote Psalm 16 found a mate for himself. He said, "You will show me the path that leads to life; your presence fills me with joy and brings me pleasure forever." The psalm writer was happy because he had found a mate. He found someone he liked to be with. Do you know who it was? It was God.

Listen to what he said: "You will show me the path that leads to life." God is the only one who shows us the way to life. He has sent Jesus to be the way, the truth, and the life for us. The psalmist also said, "Your presence . . . brings me pleasure forever." We can enjoy being with other people. But only God can promise to be with us forever.

You and God are a pair—like these two socks are a pair. Since you match God that means you do not match those who do not match him. Earlier the same psalm said, "Those who rush to other gods bring many troubles on themselves. I will not take part in their sacrifices; I will not worship their gods" (v. 4). The psalmist knew he would not be happy with those who went away from God. You do not belong with those who deny God. You are not a pair with them.

However, when you are a match with God, you are also a match with others who belong to him. In the verse I first read to you the psalmist said that being with God filled him with joy. He also wrote, "How excellent are the Lord's faithful people! My greatest pleasure is to be with them" (v. 3).

Jesus showed us he liked to be with us when he came to live on earth. Even after he died to pay for our sins, he came back. He promised to be with us forever. Because he likes to be with us, we like to be with him. When we are with Jesus, we are also with one another and with others who love Jesus.

I like being with you. I am glad Jesus is with us.

God Remembers to Make You Remember

THE WORD

The Lord does not let us forget his wonderful actions;
he is kind and merciful.
He provides food for those who have reverence for him;
he never forgets his covenant.

Psalm 111:4-5
(Twenty-Seventh Sunday after Pentecost)

THE WORLD

A travel alarm clock or a wristwatch with an alarm

Matt and his father were going on a trip together. They had to get up early in the morning to catch an airplane. Both of them overslept. They missed the plane and did not get to take the trip.

That's a sad story. Maybe you have missed something because you forgot to be at the right place at the right time. If you have, you know how disappointed you can be. Sometimes we forget what we are supposed to do. We even forget important things.

Now let's change the story a little. Matt and his father are going on a trip. Matt's father sets his alarm *(do it)* to wake him up on time. When the alarm goes off the father gets up. Matt hears the alarm too; he also gets up. Because the father had the alarm set for himself both of them got up on time and they went on their trip together.

The story of Matt and his father is a parable about you and God. God wants to live with you. That's why he sent his Son Jesus to be a part of your family. But sometimes you, like me and everyone else, forget that Jesus is a part of your life. Just as Matt overslept and missed his trip, you can forget that Jesus wants to go with you in every part of your life.

Even though you may forget Jesus, Jesus does not forget you. Psalm 111 tells us, "[God] never forgets his covenant." God is like Matt's father. He has an alarm that wakes him up. His alarm is not a clock. It is his love for us that keeps him alert. Because he loves us he never forgets us. Even when Jesus suffered on the cross to pay for our sins, he did not forget us. Even then he asked God to forgive those who had forgotten who he was.

The psalm tells us God will not forget us. But listen to what else it says: "The Lord does not let us forget his wonderful actions; he is kind and merciful. He provides food for those who have reverence for him." God remembers us and he also helps us remember him. Matt's father set the alarm so he would wake up. But the alarm also woke up Matt. God has the love that keeps him alert to take care of us. But his love also keeps us alert. When God remembers to love us, his love reminds us to love him.

When we see the good things God has done for us, we cannot forget him. The psalm reminds you that your food is a gift from God. Each time you eat, remember to thank God for the gift of food. Then think of all the other gifts that God has given you. He never forgets you. When you know this you can never forget him.

A King Forever

THE WORD

The Lord is king.
He is clothed with majesty and strength.
The earth is set firmly in place and cannot be moved.
Your throne, O Lord, has been firm from the
beginning,
and you existed before time began.

Psalm 93:1-2
(Christ the King—Last Sunday after Pentecost)

THE WORLD

Five identical empty cans (soft drink or food cans) on
a board. Glue or nail one of the cans to the board.

See these five cans? *(Show them.)* You may look at
them but not touch them. One is different than the
others. Can you see the difference? They are all the
same size. They are all empty. They are all the same
color and have the same words on them. The difference is not some little mark or dent. It is a big
difference.

You can see the difference when I show you. *(Turn
the board over so four of the cans fall.)* Now you see
the difference. One can is fastened to the board. The
other four were sitting on the board. They all looked
the same when I held the board still. But when I
turned it over, you could see the difference.

Remember those cans and listen to part of Psalm
93: "The Lord is king. He is clothed with majesty and
strength. The earth is set firmly in place and cannot be
moved. Your throne, O Lord, has been firm from the
beginning, and you existed before time began."

126

The psalm says the Lord is a king. He dresses like a king and he sits on a throne like a king. But there are many other kings. The other kings also dress like kings and sit on thrones. But there is a big difference between the Lord and the other kings. The difference is not in what they wear or the thrones they sit on. The difference is that the Lord has a throne that has been firm from the beginning. The other kings come and the other kings go. But the Lord is our king forever. He existed before time began. He will exist after time ends. He is like the can that is fastened to the board. That can did not fall off when the board was tipped over. God does not fall away from us when we have problems. He is our king forever.

We do not have other kings today. But we do have other things that are important to us. *(Put the other cans back on the board.)* Think of these cans as the things that are important to you. This is your family. This is your health. This is food and clothing. This can be fun and games. Or you can think of other things that are important.

But this can *(point to the one glued to the board)* is Jesus. He has been your Savior long before any of the other things existed. Long ago he died for you and then came back to life. He is important to you now. All the other things are also important now. But they will change. They will drop away. *(Turn the board over again.)* Jesus is the king who will last forever.